SUCCESS
THROUGH
SELF EVALUATION

SUCCESS
THROUGH
SELF EVALUATION

THINK AND ACT DIFFERENTLY FOR SUCCESS

Dr. Abhilash Chembath

PARTRIDGE

A Penguin Random House Company

To order additional copies of this book, contact
Partridge India
000 800 10062 62
orders.india@partridgepublishing.com

www.partridgepublishing.com/india

Contents

Acknowledgements

To my wife Nisha. K, son Sreevardhan, my father Sri. C.A.Sukumaran.

To my mother Late Smt. O.N.Leela, mother's elder sister Late Smt. Padmavathi Amma and Smt. Saraswathi Amma and my uncle Sri. O.N.Ramakrishnan, my aunty Smt. Girija amma who always loved and cared me, and helped me all the way long.

To my Uma teacher and Sasikumar Sir who helped me to edit it.

To my brother Mr. O.R.Roopesh who helped me to design my cover page.

To my workplaces and organizations which gave me sufficient inputs through live examples.

To all my colleagues who supported me through good and bad experiences.

To all of my colleagues and friends and well wishers.

The reasons for writing this book

After my education, while working through various fields in various industries including MNC's, I felt a huge gap between me and others. I began to think, why it happened, or happens always. At last I could find an answer for that. It is nothing but, due to the frequency mismatch between two aspects-one was me and the other would obviously be my work place colleagues and bosses. Very less I could find human values inside companies. There occurred only filthy business making techniques, without sticking to any of the human values.

Contrary, I always found a humanitarian aspect in each and every problem. Due to the system of actions possessed by bosses and others, many people started feeling very bad, and ended up in deep remorse, which ended up in even quitting their jobs as well. Nobody was there to support them on personal and humanitarian grounds. But, I used to. As a result, even I was sent out. Thus, I thought why not there be some guidelines in handling people-whether it is bosses, subordinates, spouses, family members, friends, relatives etc.

Also, since I am in the helping field through Counselling, I use to encounter people problems-inside family, between friends, couple, relatives etc. It might include some psychiatric issues as well – but not always. At times, simple egos and complexes also shattered people relationships. Sometimes exaggerations, magnifications, distortion of thoughts or messages were also found to be prominent in shattering relationships.

As a result, I have included living situations and examples in this book. With that, possible suggestions and modifications in current thought processes and attitudes are being mentioned in this book. Also, basic parameters towards success achievement are also mentioned thereafter. People always focus on criticizing others, point towards others' mistakes and all. So I thought, there need to be a reverse process. Instead of criticizing others and situations, why can't we first of all evaluate ourselves, was a thought made me write this book. Such a thought inspired and drove me in putting all those in these words.

The deterioration of morals, ethics, values etc. from the society is yet another alarming factor, which need an escalation and correction. True love is yet another deteriorating aspect from the world. Everything is getting materialized, and human relationships get lessened and lessened day by day. There need to be a change in that aspect also. People just run behind money, but for many reasons, they forget enjoying with that money, and at a later stage, they spend those moneys to recoup their health which they lost, for making money. People are getting converted into money minting machines only. There values are getting degraded.

So, my dear friends, this is going to be really an eye opener and guide to begin your journey towards success.

So, my sincere request to you is that, please open your eyes and ears to the outside world, to hear good news about the success of you as well as that of your beloved ones. It is intended to cater to the needs of all segments in the society independent of age, gender, occupation etc.

I wish you all the very best to achieve great success in life.

Chapter 1

Introduction

Most people fail to succeed due to their low morality and less self confidence. There comes the problem of attitude as well as beliefs and values. Then comes the question, 'how to overcome main enemies of success?' The answer is so simple - just impart good morality and self confidence, built up with attitude and good moral values. Doesn't it sound simple? But, is it that simple? If it's that simple, why do people fail? It seems to be a very relevant question. Remember Newton's law "For each and every action, there is an equal and opposite reaction". It simply means, 'what you sow, so you reap', in our practical life. How do we relate Newton's law with our life? Does is sound confusing? Don't worry; **we shall discuss this in a later part of this book in detail**. Simply put, what we do, will reflect back on us. Our good deeds will reap good results and vice versa.

To succeed in life, one ought to have the real thrive for it. You need to learn to generate a burning desire in you. You need to adopt many factors put together to build the big baggage of success. Human beings are products of their previous life experiences. What makes room for success is one's attitude. Success and failure are made by us. Thus, attitude building is a very important factor in one's life as well as profession. To become a successful person, you need to learn to build positive attitude. We will discuss it on the way.

Ideas are important too. Good ideas will drive you in a direction where you meet success.

You cannot succeed without knowledge. Knowledge can come from anywhere. You have to be very keen to receive it from any means. Knowledge building is as important as attitude and self confidence. **We will discuss in detail, how all these things are interconnected, just like members of a family**.

You should be able to build your personality through your own ways. One person's ideas can influence the other too. Thus, you may try to follow the successful ones, not in full, but to an extent. If you try to follow someone blindly, you will become genuinely blind. You will lose your identity as well, and you will surrender your personality before someone, which should not happen in your life.

It is often said that when a rabbit starts imitating an elephant in its eating habits, it will really suffer. If you try to blindly imitate Arnold Schwarzenegger's performance in a body show, you may end up in frustration and sometimes even in depression. You will have to learn about his past, how he became successful in his area and so on before you start imitating him. You will have to ask yourself first whether it is really viable for you.

You may be confused about measurement criteria. **We will discuss about this also in this book**.

I wish you all the best and thank you for referring this book, "Success Through Self Evaluation". If you have any suggestion, please do not be hesitant to post it in the given address. Once again I wish you all the best in your work as well as in your life.

Self Evaluation is nothing but the measurement of one's self. It is a comparison of one's past, present and future by oneself, as well as a study of oneself from the feedback of others, thus making an evaluation of oneself or self-evaluation. To do so, you need to adopt some simple techniques, **which will be discussed later**.

We will also discuss about the concepts of love and respect and what's there in common between these two.

Chapter 2

The Value of Self Evaluation

Self evaluation is the process of collecting and analyzing relevant information about oneself. The information can be from external factors also, in the form of feed back from others.

Self evaluation is said to be done when you become aware of your interests, personality traits, skills, values, and beliefs and also of your limitations and fears. Based on these, you can generate your own interests, pave your own way to success and thus become your own boss. Then you will decide where you want to be and what you want to be. You need to try to ask the following questions to yourself. What do I like? What is important to me? What am I good at? **It will be discussed later in detail**.

The evaluation process takes various means or modes. Firstly it may be the evaluation of **objects** or materials. Secondly there comes the evaluation of **situations**, thirdly, the evaluation of other **people**, and finally the so called **self**-evaluation, upon which I would like to throw some light.

Evaluation of objects

For every thing to occur in a fine mode/mood, a certain type of evaluation is required. It will be just like conducting examinations at academies, taking performance reports periodically, making verifications, evaluating performances, holding examinations to evaluate the knowledge of students. This will help the teachers to decide the proficiency of the students at all levels. In organizations, financial auditing is done to analyze and evaluate the fund position, sales meetings are done to evaluate sales performance or figures. All these types of activities are done to evaluate some thing or somebody, to find out or measure their capacity or capability. If a new plan or strategy is incorporated by an organization, it also needs to be measured, to evaluate its success ratio. If a new car is released by a company, it also has to be test driven, or tested several times in captivity as well as in real time situations. Similarly, if a new concept is to be incorporated, it also has to be thoroughly evaluated before implementation. Also, in the long run, after the implementation of new products or ideas, periodic evaluation and assessment has to be done to measure the productivity or result making capacity, what we call efficiency. Thus, evaluation is an inevitable thing in all perspectives.

Evaluation of situations

Evaluation takes many forms. There comes a story into my mind. There was a doctor and his student. Once they both went to treat a lord who was suffering from severe gastritis. After diagnosing the disease and prescribing suitable medicine, the doctor asked the lord whether he had eaten banana. On hearing the doctor's question the lord answered in the positive. The student who was with the doctor was really amazed that the doctor had clearly found out that the lord did have a banana even though he did not ask anything about it earlier, and assumed that his boss, the doctor was having some sort of supernatural power of knowing things correctly.

After getting out of the palace, the student praised the doctor about his wisdom. Then the doctor replied, "You fool! It is not any sort of supernatural power, but just common sense". But the student simply could not understand how he found out the matter that the lord had a banana even though he did not ask the lord about it before prescribing the medicine. He was not ready to withdraw from it. He was restless and frustrated till he know the truth about the matter. He again asked the doctor about it. Then the doctor answered "Didn't you notice a banana peel lying under the cot on which the lord was lying? I just assumed that the lord might have eaten the banana and asked him about it, and got the right answer.

The student helper really was interested in his boss and worked along with him. Some months passed. One day, the prince of his territory was suffering from severe fever. The doctor was not at station, and the student went to attend the case along with his junior. He acted as the senior, our student wanted to shine before his junior and wanted to show him that he was a very experienced one than his junior.

After examining the prince, he asked the prince whether he had some grass for breakfast. He was trying to imitate his senior doctor and tried to apply his commonsense keeping in mind the previous incident of banana peel. On hearing the question, the prince slapped him and ordered to put him behind the bars. When the doctor heard the news, he came to the palace. He spoke to the prince and took necessary steps to release his student.

Once the student was released, the doctor asked him about the matter. He explained the situation to the doctor. He justified that what he did was right, and he only followed his boss doctor, of assuming things, and only imitated the doctor's method. The doctor asked him to explain the incident. Thus he started explaining the incident. There was a piece of grass under the cot on which the prince was lying. Seeing this he asked the prince whether he had grass for breakfast. He justified himself that he didn't do anything wrong, but just imitated his boss.

This story throws light on the fact that that you need to evaluate and analyze things and situations, and without just imitating somebody, you need to use your discretionary power and analytical skill before coming to conclusions. In our story, the student could have avoided the adverse situation if he had used his discretionary power. Evaluation of situations takes different means. It has a variety of manifestations, and everything depends on specific cases. We cannot generalize them as we do it always.

This is an instance of the evaluation occurring outside our self, but related to our mind and our self. This is entirely different from the pure external evaluation, or evaluation which is not at all related directly to us. For instance, the evaluation of others or other objects.

Thus we have seen different types of evaluations like external, which are not related to us directly, like physical objects, other persons not related to us etc. There are some cases where we may have to evaluate ourselves, which we can term as **self evaluation**. Unless and until we compare us with ourselves, we cannot evaluate us, and through the evaluation process only we can develop.

Evaluation of people

Each employee of an organization will be put under training or probation for a certain period of time, to evaluate his/her performance. This is to affirm his position if doing well, or sack him out, if found not up to the mark. At times, we a may also evaluate somebody or something for no reason. For example we estimate or underestimate people or things in many ways, either knowingly or unknowingly. While discussing this point, an epic story comes into my mind.

One day the great scholar Sri Sankaracharya was on a journey. On the way he met a tribal man with a dog coming opposite to him. Sankaracharya being a deified person was arrogant with the other man, whom he underestimated. He began to scold the man asking how he dared to stand on the way of such a great person like himself. The tribal man stood still till Sankaracharya completed his words against him.

After hearing all those bad words from Sankaracharya, the tribal man told him that, such a great person like Sankaracharya shouldn't have even thought about a matter like this regarding caste and creed. He again told him that a person like Sankaracharya needs to inspire others to put an end to caste and creed discrimination, and not follow it as he did with him. The tribal man's words really opened his eyes. After that, Sankaracharya fell on the feet of the tribal man and asked for forgiveness. By that time, the tribal man had taken the form of Lord Siva. Lord Siva was on to testing Sankaracharya by transforming himself to a tribal man. The story reminds us that we should not underestimate any one, nor should we evaluate others in a wrong way.

We cannot evaluate a person by just seeing him/her physically. We need to understand the person in detail. Then only can we evaluate him/her. There are some people who tell that they can assess a person by just having a look at his/her face. They pretend to be experts in face reading and at last end up in trouble.

There is also an instance which throws light on this issue, from my own life. While I was going to Bangalore from Chennai on an official purpose by bus, a not so good looking person came and sat next to me. He was having a long beard, and wearing an old jubbah. At first sight, one would hesitate to sit next to a person like him. I initially thought of shifting to another seat. But there was no seat vacant.

I tried to reconcile to the situation and sat in the same seat. Before the bus started, a team of people got into the bus. Soon after they entered into the bus, I saw them coming towards me. I was happy and about to get up to welcome them. But as soon as they reached by my seat, they started offering their hands to the person sitting beside me. Only then did I know that they had really come to see the person sitting beside and not me.

While going through a magazine on reaching Bangalore the very next day, I found the picture of the same person who sat beside me in it and the people who entered the bus later. Later I could understand that he was the director of the newly shot film in Kannada which was a super hit, and the team belonged to his group.

I was really embarrassed thinking about the whole incident and was really ashamed of myself being so silly and not even trying to utter a word to him. I thought that if I had spoken to him at least once, one day I also might have become a film person writing not books but stories and screen plays. The estimation and evaluation of people may take different means. It may not be as simple as telling somebody about something which doesn't cater any meaning.

I know some air hostesses telling that they have great experience of meeting different types of people each day, with different characters, varied prejudices, different behaviors. Some might be friendly, some hard, some so gentle, some so cute, some rough and many more. Such an experience gives an airhostess a learning on evaluating people.

There are sales guys also who have similar experiences. I too when training sales team, used to meet at least 15 different types of 'prospects', as said above, with different characters and different behavioral patterns. The same experience really added to my knowledge base in a practical way. All the things I learned in life really came from that sales experience. The specialty and uniqueness of knowledge is that, as you give more, it multiplies more. It's like the flame of a lamp or candle. The things I know, I am trying to share with you.

Self evaluation

Self evaluation is the area I wish to highlight in this book. As this gives us a clear picture of ourselves, we must rely upon this. The "Success Through Self-evaluation" will give you a real awareness of yourself. After understanding the core values of the same, you will become a new personality, because a huge part of your personality relies upon self-evaluation. If you learn to evaluate yourselves, you become your own boss.

The foundation of self evaluation starts from the basic idea of one's own knowledge. Your experience with yourself is equivalent to your age. That is, you know yourself better than any one else on the earth. Your perception, your experience etc will be an asset to know yourself, your own understanding by yourself. Thus nobody on the earth can know you as much as you know yourselves. You are the only person eligible to evaluate yourself. Here starts your work of the self-evaluation. Keeping this in your mind, you begin to think about your performance, achievements etc. **The easy way of evaluating yourself will be discussed later**.

Self evaluation starts with the comparison of your own status, performance, skills, behavior, actions, thoughts etc with the same parameters in your past. One's present position in comparison to one's past is the criterion for self-evaluation. You need to begin to position yourself successfully. If you do it with more pace, you will succeed or else be lost. I give you a clue for self evaluation process. You have succeeded in self-evaluation when you make an assessment of yourself with respect to where you were (past), where you are (present), and where you will be (future).

To know yourself, you need to ask the following questions to yourself, as discussed earlier. What do I like? What is important to me? What am I good at? The following questions about yourself will help you improve yourself. You need to analyze about the following:

Interests

Identifying and acknowledging your interests will help you decide which occupations/stream of study/subjects/ college to look to and possibly pursue. Therefore, ask yourself: What do I take pleasure in? What do I enjoy?

Personality

How do you interact with the world? Where do you direct your energy? What kind of information do you naturally notice? How do you make decisions? The answers to these types of questions reflect different aspects of your personality. Depending on your particular personality traits, you will prefer certain occupations over others.

Skills

Skills are your abilities and areas of strength that are learned through many different activities, including work, extracurricular and volunteering experiences, and hobbies. You can discover what your skills are by becoming aware of those things that you do well.

Values

What is important to you? The answer to this question will be a determining factor when deciding upon an occupational field. Examples include: "Making use of your abilities," "Being Rich" "Being Famous" "Being busy all the time," or "Working alone."

Beliefs

Beliefs are positive or negative thoughts you hold about yourself. Your self assessment will influence the career goals you set and the actions you take towards achieving such goals.

Details about similar **factors will be discussed in relevant areas in this book**.

For everyone or everything to be improved, one must be so emotionally as well as physically involved in the process of doing so. Two most important factors are needed to develop and maintain this: "*Continuous improvement*" or "*Kaizen*", and "*Learning*". If one sticks on to these two important concepts, success comes naturally. It will also sustain. The concept of *kaizen* will be immediately discussed and *learning* will be discussed at Knowledge section.

Application of Kaizen

I think most of you may be aware of the term "Kaizen". Don't worry even if not so. I will help you to understand what it is. It's a Japanese term, which means "change for the better". You should be able to impart changes in your work as well as life. A lion's share of our time is spent on work, thus our life means work also. If we start imparting change in our life, work will also be improved and vice versa.

You may be confused with the term simply "change". But it has to be understood in only a positive sense. You need to impart changes in your work as well as life in a positive way. You need to improve day by day. The term Kaizen just cannot be explained in a very simple sense. Each and every aspect of our life need to be influenced by Kaizen.

We all know that Japan is a super power in the world. Soon after the destruction of Japan by Americans, it developed drastically. It was solely due to the hard work of the people of Japan to recreate their nation. The patriotism exhibited by them deserves to be appreciated. Day and night they worked very hard to rebuild their nation.

The level of patriotism exhibited by them and the rate of hard work each and every person had done, from children to the aged must be appreciated. They still work for their nation first. To work for oneself is only of secondary importance to them. That's the spirit of the Japanese.

We must really be ashamed of ourselves. What's there extraordinary about the Japanese? Are there any extra natural resources with them? They live amidst volcanoes, not greenery. There's a saying that you need to live like Japanese. This saying was generated out of the strain and pain suffered by each and every citizen of Japan. **If each and every citizen of developing countries begins to think like that, we cannot just imagine where our world will stand.**

There are many instances where we should appreciate them. They start their work right from 7 in the morning till late at night. They all work for the contentment they achieve through the development of their nation. What we must learn from them is their dedicated and sincere hard work, not blocking work through strikes and the greed to make more for less work. The real contentment they enjoy through their achievements might be applauded. They really are ready to work more and more. That is why each and every person round the globe asks for and prefer Japanese products. They strive for quality in their products. There are sharp differences between Japanese made products and products from other countries. People go for them because of their quality and performance aspect. We perceive them with a sort of guarantee that Japanese products are superior to others. Things have taken such a shape because of the positive outlook and perseverance of the Japanese.

Kaizen implies a way of thinking and behaving. Thus we must improve our thoughts first. **We will discuss later how it can be done**. The change for the better need to be continuous. You should not stop the process by thinking that you have developed. It is a big mistake, if you think like that. No body in the world is perfect. Everybody is in the process of change and development. The rate and pace with which a person develops, paves the way for his/her own success.

The faster you develop, the sooner you meet success. Once you start imparting the so called positive change, you will start feeling the changes happening to you. For that the first clue will be to bring changes continuously, with your hard effort first. Then later you will feel the changes coming to you automatically.

There was an incident in my life. While I was working at Calicut, I was in search of a house to stay with my family. I sought the help of the company authorities. But it didn't turn fruitful. They however arranged a hostel accommodation. There were already four guys in the room. The management of the hostel told me that if I was interested, they would provide an extra cot, and I could stay there.

It didn't suit me. The entire atmosphere didn't look good and I felt suffocated there. What I did was to ring a friend at the local place, who was normally not at station. To God's grace, at that time, he was available. He asked me to wait there and soon he reached. It was around 10.30 pm. I went along with him and stayed at his house that night.

The next morning I was dropped at the bus stop from where I could catch a bus to my new office. For ten to fifteen minutes, no bus came towards that side. I missed some auto rickshaws too. Finally I decided to take an auto rickshaw and move to the office.

On the way I just mentioned the driver about my need for a house. Luckily he was a person with some contacts, even at the political level. He introduced me to a local broker who found me a house next to my office. I still find this incident as the stated reversal of the good deeds I had done. That is the positive change reverted to myself. There are many instances in my life, where I found God before me in many forms.

The next incident is very interesting. I had met with two bus accidents within a span of three months. In the first one, the bus I was traveling in fell into a paddy field, which was muddy and marshy due to the morning shower.

It was around fifteen feet deep. What I do remember was the sudden jerk and the resultant sound.

It was within a fraction of a second. By the time I realized the matter, every thing was over. I was covered in mud and looked murky. I was finding it very hard to raise my left hand, as the left collar bone was paining like any thing. By evaluating the nature of the accident, anything could have occurred. Luckily I broke only my left collar bone and there was nothing grave or dangerous to worry about. Many people were seriously injured. Looking at the severity of the accident, anything could have happened. God was with me as a savior.

Thus each and every one of us have to wake up and try to bring changes in our life, the very positive changes.

Before I explain Kaizen, we need to apply it in a more simple way. If you start applying Kaizen in your each and every action, you will make success your comrade. Application of Kaizen brings changes in your life as well as your surroundings. There is a saying that if you are good, your family will be good. If your family is good, your neighbor will be good. If your neighbor is good, your society will be good, and if your society is good, your nation will be good.

There was an instance while I was working at Trivandrum, in sales and marketing training of a multi national company. We were a team of 6 members, residing at a remote village, as part of a campaign. The area was very bad and the people residing there were quite uncultured. The one family residing opposite to our residence was our head ache for days. I say this because, they were disturbing our sleep and taught us very bad words. They were very unruly and used abusive language. They were a big pain and altogether disturbed our peace.

Every night the family head came on six legs. You will be confused how a person could come on six legs. The remaining four legs were that of the persons who were carrying him up to his house. That is, two persons were carrying him on their shoulders to his house. This person had a very bad habit of scolding first those who carried him, when he saw the door of his house, then his wife and children, and so on. We used to sleep daily listening to ugly words, and after some days, we got used to it. The same things were repeated in the morning also. Every day we woke up listening to the foul words of that man. We were thinking of the condition of their children when they grow up.

Unknowingly we were induced with a sense of the bad and the ugly. It will happen to everybody who is supposed to face such an incident. If the neighbor is a priest, who prays god at least two times a day, we could have heard the devotional songs, prayers etc., and we could have smelled the holy smoke. Then our personality would have been bettered positively. Unknowingly we would have at least thought of God and related things.

This is the implication of the change which we would hold when we are approached to good and bad things or situations. In the Indian language, Sanskrit, there is a term called "Satsanga" which means being with good ones and making good people your companions. So always try to be with good people, good situations, good environment, and everything good. Always create and retain good friends. Thus you need to be aware that "friendship is not collection of hearts, but selection of hearts". To become yourself good, please do bear in mind that you are only with good people. One can either create or destroy a person.

There was a person who spent his whole life, putting his heart and soul to serve the society even at the cost of his own family life. He sacrificed his wife's and children's pleasures too. After spending one whole lifetime, he came to know that, such a revamping of the society is highly difficult or, to simply put it, impossible. By the time he came to understand this fact, he had almost lost his whole life. Now he recognized that, the change should start from his own home. If one's home is changed, the neighbourhood could be changed, if one's neighbourhood is changed, the locality could be changed, and so on and so forth which would lead to the change / reformation of the entire country or the world, over a period of time.

We all have to initiate the change from our own home itself. Our home should be filled with love and joy. It has to be filled with pleasure and leisure, and what not. This would reflect in the entire world, if each and everyone does this, and we need not depend on anybody else for peace of mind.

I came across many people who have been destroyed by their colleagues or friends. The basic nature of certain people is to exploit others. They pretend to be friends and try to cheat. Thus, while selecting a friend, you need to be vigilant. You may get many friends, but a productive one is very rare. As the saying, "a friend in need is a friend indeed". This throws light really to a sincere friend who stands along with us at our good and bad times.

We need to remember the story of two friends which we learned in our kindergarten classes. Two friends were going through a forest. On the way they came to see a bear. It was coming towards them so furiously. What one of them did was to climb upon a tree and tried to safeguard only his life. He forgot about the other one's life. But, the other one was intelligent enough and pretended dead, and lay down on the ground still, as if dead. The bear approached him, smelled him and left him alone, thinking that he was dead.

When the bear left that place, the one who was up the tree slowly came down and asked his friend if he was safe. He just told him goodbye forever and struck him off from his friend's list. This story is really important in selecting friends, and understanding them if selected. Those who stand with you at all times will be your real comrades. So you will be lucky if you have a friend like a comrade, with you all times.

He will not only help you, but be with you. Likewise, you are also liable to help him. What you get will have to be delivered back. Then only will the two sides be bridged. Care and help has to be two sided and not one sided. There are certain instances where you may have to help people without urging for return. Then the picture will be entirely different. We may be assuming a great role over there. As told in the holy bible, "what you wish others to do for you, you do it for them".

There comes the action where you exhibit the sort of service to others, without seeking back anything. By doing so, you will be freed from all sorts of tensions or stress. As told by the great Buddha, you have worries, if you love something or somebody beyond the limit. You should set limit to anything you do or act, which need to be very clearly set. **This we will discuss later**.

By Kaizen we need to focus on improvement, not innovation. There was an incident at a colony where I was residing in the course of my sales training job. There was one nice neighbour, whom I used to interact with very much. He was a person who could talk endlessly about anything under the sun.

He was having an old scooter, which was not likely to have been serviced so far. It made so much noise that you could not stand it for even a minute.

The above said person was a healthy guy. Did he have any exercise? Did he ever go for a walk? Did he go to a gymnasium? Did he swim? Had he ever run? To your surprise, he didn't do anything stated above. Still you will be confused how he was keeping himself fit. I will tell you. This was due to his old scooter.

You may be thinking how a scooter can help maintain one's health. You might have heard that by possessing a vehicle, you abstain from walking and lose your health. His scooter helped him out to solve his health problem. I am reducing the curiosity knot. I will tell you how. It's really interesting. Every time he stops his vehicle or starts his vehicle, he might have to do it at least half an hour.

By kicking the scooter for such a long time, he had sufficient exercise and thus maintained his health, by burning the fat. Thus his scooter, unlike other bad ones, helped his owner keep fit. My attempt here is to differentiate the terms 'improvement' and 'innovation'.

I used to tell him always to repair his old scooter at least or to dispose it and buy a new one. But he always replied he would buy a new car, and was least bothered of the junk scooter. Instead of cursing the poor old vehicle, he could have maintained it at least by repairing it. But he never did it and kept on cursing the old scooter.

Here we come to understand that the person in our incident always looks or believes in what would happen or occur, and not what is happening, and relies upon anticipations or dreams alone. Instead, he could have repaired the old vehicle. This is called as innovation. Had he repaired the vehicle, it would have meant that he believed on improvement.

What we come to understand is that, we need to maintain what we possess. Otherwise, it will become a burden for us. Just for name's sake we might possess something. But we should never be like that. As in the stated incident, we need to never rely upon anticipation, but reality.

There are some people who use mobile phones without sufficient credit balance to make calls in it. Whenever some need arises to make a call, they seek some other's phones usually. Then why are they carrying a phone? They could have discarded it. If we possess something, it should be useful to us. Otherwise why carry a burden with us unnecessarily. Similarly, there are people who scare the police while driving their vehicles. They might run short of adequate statutory records like license, insurance papers or RC book. When we reside in a country where the law demands so, we should strictly abide by the same, otherwise we should not drive or own vehicles. If you cannot do such simple things, why should you drive it? It is as simple as that.

Thus, I think you have come to understand about the difference between improvement and innovation. Thus by the application of Kaizen, you need to learn to make use of the **resources** you have. You need to be able to utilize the facility you have. Whatever you possess should be value added, and readily available for use. Otherwise keeping a burden may be avoided.

Thus, if you start applying Kaizen in your system, you will result in increased productivity. There was an incident where I asked one of my students whether he started applying Kaizen, he answered lightly that he didn't get time for that. How ridiculous is his attitude! Does any one require a separate time to apply Kaizen? It's a continuous process in each and every second of our life and is a part of our breath. Then only would we develop. You need to bear in mind the very meaning of the term Kaizen-"Change for the better, or change for betterment".

Another implication of Kaizen is to get the work done effectively with less cost. Thus we need to keep in mind the usage "Cheap and best". It doesn't mean that you have to possess a posh vehicle, a posh house, very expensive food, dandy dress, costly holiday trips etc. Whatever you possess need to be simple and readily available.

There are some people who walk around so colourful and dandy, and never help anyone. You need not be like that, at least after reading this book, or evaluating yourselves. Only by helping others through any of the possible ways, we could get help from others as well. What I mean is, everyone cannot be like rich people who shower money and other things to the needy or, just waste them. We have to do our level best in helping others in the best possible way. Only giving opens the way to getting. It is like a gradient or a flow channel. Unless and until you give, you will not get anything, as the flow channel is not continuous and blocked. Thus, practice helping and giving, to better your life and others' life through you. It is my advice to the readers to have a "Give and Get" policy.

There are certain firms which are least bothered about the competitors, and at last end up in failure. As they are least bothered about the competitor strength, they cannot really perform well. Only if they apply Kaizen, can they survive, lest somebody else will steal the show. They need to be more bothered about their weaknesses rather than their strengths. What happened with the two giants IBM and GM (General Motors)? Are you aware about where these two giants have disappeared? Were they so weak companies? Even they were almost out from the market.

Can you guess why such a thing happened to them? They thought they were the only ones strong in their industry. Thus they didn't do proper marketing at a point of time when many other companies with advanced classes of similar products were launched. The giants didn't mind them and misinterpreted that the new ones were just kids and they were not going to harm them.

But the picture turned the other way. When they woke up on a fine morning, the market was full of new products from the new companies. The new ones were able to conquer the market especially the heart of the customers, through new designs which the customers were urging. So far they were seeing the same old models and designs. But when the new designs were brought in front of them, they were really surprised and joined hands with the new ones who actually made their dreams a reality.

They wanted a change from the very traditional designs and models. The old "Ambassador" cars in India from GM and big computers from IBM were totally discarded by the customers, i.e. market. They went behind the new ones for beauty, design and comfort. The style and posh features offered by the new ones grabbed the hearts of people in all senses. They just went behind them. They didn't do any mistake, did they? Never.

Similar will be case with us also. Unless we perform well, we will face all sorts of problems. Thus to avoid problems, you need to perform well. Are you getting me? What I wish to express is, there is no other way to meet success than to perform well. "Only the performers will persist, others will perish". This slogan you must keep in mind. This reminds us of the scientific theory of "struggle for existence" and "survival of the fittest". For this we need to "Focus" first and foremost upon our responsibilities. There are only two options before us. Either Do or Die is to face the reality.

What this means is as follows: In the process of evolution, many weak organisms were out from the earth. They were defeated and overcome by the strongest ones. Thus the strongest ones began to rule the earth. The same happened with dinosaurs and many others. Thus they were completely swept out from the earth and into that slot, came many other strong organisms. This shows the meaning of the two theories stated above.

In short it might be explained that the weaker ones will always be thrown out and suppressed by the stronger ones. If General Motors and IBM were aware of this fact and acted appropriately, they would never fail and themselves would have been the leaders even in the present scenario. Same could occur with us too. If we perform less, we are out from the scene. Thus, for us to stick on to the competitive environment, we need to perform to the core and make a land mark.

Coming back again to Japan, there is an interesting story regarding the result and performance of Japanese. There was an incident where a prominent American computer giant once went for a deal with a Japanese company, on the way to development. The American company put orders for a certain commodity for certain numbers. At the end of the purchase order they didn't forget to write "there should be only maximum three defective pieces per thousand of the stated commodity". They thus mentioned the complaint/defect rate.

The Japanese, after referring to the purchase order, and sending the ordered commodity, enclosed a note with their sale letter / invoice. It read "as per your purchase order, we herewith enclose the stated number of commodities. Along with them, three defective pieces have been **separately manufactured** and enclosed. We thought it's mandatory". Lucky that the American computer giant did have the common sense not to relate with a company in a developing nation. Here lies the difference between Japan and other countries. Each and everyone has to sit and analyze this point before doing an action.

As you start applying Kaizen you start saving time, money, energy and many more. Thus you evaluate each and every second, where you have applied **Continuous Improvement.** If not, start it from now itself. There is only 24 hours in everyone's watch, be it that of Mr. Obama or yours or of myself. But think about what had made the difference. It is not the time, but, the effective utilization of time and nothing else. Friends, let us not waste the most valuable time, save it and utilize it; as we all know, time is more precious, and we waste it more.

Easy way of self evaluation

Every day you will be in touch with many people, many activities and so on. Each time you will be performing or underperforming. Daily before you go to sleep, make a habit of dreaming or visualizing the activities of the whole day. Each and every aspect needs to be reviewed. Repeat this for at least two weeks. Then you will find out which are the areas where you perform and under perform. You will be able to point out the common areas of strengths and weaknesses on your side.

The thought processes are to involve the detailed visualization of your day to day activities. From that you need to be able to analyze where you are strong and where you are weak. For example, if you find everyone is getting annoyed with you frequently, then analyze the areas where it occurs. After that, you try to resolve the problem, by thorough self study as well as seeking feedbacks from the concerned.

For that, first of all you need to find out the problem and record it very personally. Then, analyze it properly, and monitor it to the core. You then compare it with yourself. The reason why most of the people get annoyed with you might be due to a variety of factors like your way of approach, your way of talking, the use of words or even slang.

Then after two weeks, you will be able to write down the common strengths and weaknesses in a personal diary. After that you will learn to analyze the common areas where you are good and bad. Then, go through the record you have maintained, stating the common strengths and weaknesses. Keep in mind that the process is very personal and never disclose it to any one, even to the dearest ones.

Now, you have found out your areas of interest, i.e. strengths and weaknesses. It's crystal clear that you have a multitude of problems within you. What I mean to say is, you will have a similar set of problems, which is being manifested in different ways. At last, if you analyze them and put in to relevant heads, you might find those heads common, which might look like interpersonal/ intrapersonal problems, behaviour problems and so on. Just like this, try to evaluate yourself judiciously to the core of your own consciousness, without cheating yourself. You will find yourself to be a new being with new wings searching new avenues to fly up.

Now, try to rectify one by one. After each and every problem recorded in your personal diary (preferably head names as explained in last paragraph) is rectified, you may put a cross on the same. Then you will become confident of resolving a great problem on your side. A huge part of your defective side has been detected and rectified by yourself. The same will be the case with your negative aspects. Each and every negative aspect within you can definitely be rectified if you do wish so. Continue the process to the extent where you eliminate all those negative elements within you.

As explained earlier, you apply Kaizen wherever applicable. Likewise here also you do the same. You go on making improvements in your life and work. Personally when doing self evaluation also, you try to apply Kaizen. Thus you will definitely be a problem free being and free from all sorts of negative traits and turn to be a decent one, free of all sorts of hassles and problems. If done so, take it from me, you have started paving the way to your success.

After doing so, you will start feeling that you have refined and turned to be a gentle being, by discarding all levels of problems. You will feel the glory of goodness flowing towards you. All the problems you were facing are being converted to good ones. The darkness surrounding you will be dissolved and disappear completely. The newness, the freshness, the rejuvenation, the elegance, the ecstasy, all you begin to feel.

The scorching sun in your life turns to be a pleasant one with the shower of respect from others, the bliss you feel and all sorts of well being will come to you. Everything you start feeling before your senses. You will analyze that you have turned to be a new person with charms and good being flowing towards you like the cool shower accompanied by the breeze of wellbeing.

You will feel the recognition, the respect and many things more. There will be no end to explain the goodness coming to you. I personally have trained and made many people to such a refined state. They are all doing well and performing successfully. All their personal complexes were dissolved in the ocean of goodness where they are picking the pearls of success and catching the fish of opportunities. What you would have come to understand is your common weaknesses and learned how to wipe them away from your life system.

Chapter 3

The Self Identity or Brand

I guess readers are pretty much aware of the creation of their own brand or identity. In the absence of such an awareness, one feels a phenomenon called Identity Crisis. Confused? It is nothing but a confusion in your mind as to who you are. Here comes the relevance of creating our own brand before others. If you could make a difference before others, you will be seen differently as well. Why is Mount Everest famous? Why river Nile and Niagra water falls? They surely have some distinct qualities different from their counterparts. Like that, if you have an identity of your own, you will have a separate entity, which others will perceive according to your brand value. Thus, try to be different and feel the difference.

The importance of presence and non presence

There was a school in a remote village. The Head teacher, Mr. Gopal was quite famous in teaching the students mathematics. He shone as a teacher with the same vigour always. None other could deliver mathematics as beautifully as this man. There were many other teachers too who taught the same subject. But, students enjoyed his class and wished to be present in his class only.

One fine morning he got promotion and was transferred to another school. After his transfer, the students began to perform badly and their marks came down unusually low. There were lots of drop-outs too. The school management was very much disturbed and frantically searched for a way out to prevent the disaster. They were really struggling to get another right person for the post. They tried many but didn't get one like Gopal.

Every one was really disturbed by this turn of event and was caught in a tight situation. This is an instance of the importance of non presence or absence. If you are able to make your own mark and make others tell that your presence would be or has been fabulous, there comes your importance. The rate with which we are able to make others tell that we are that important, points to our success. We then make the mark that we have been successful than anyone else.

In our day to day life itself, there are situations where we make comparisons, like for instance, of the old sales manager and new one. We usually compare the two persons generally and match them with each other. The one who is outstanding will be admired and remembered in a nice way and the one who stands out will be remembered in a bad way. Each and every one of us need to be thus aware of this fact and be ready to make a good impression on others so that we will be remembered even in our absence.

Chapter 4

The importance of thoughts

For every act or event to occur, there need to be an inspiration. Without inspiration, nothing will happen. If you adopt inspiration based on good values, you will achieve good results and vice versa. Similarly, the value and importance of thought comes into the scene. For example, your vehicle needs fuel to run. Otherwise, there is no meaning in keeping a vehicle, is there? Likewise, you have to water your apple tree to get apples from it. You have to punish softly your children, to make them grow up as good individuals. You will have to propel the aero plane, for it to rise in the air. You will have to propel the ship to move it, and the examples are many. But, why don't we apply all these things into our own lives? Great people have succeeded through great ideas, which come out of great thoughts. **We will discuss about ideas later**.

Thoughts are our driving force. As Buddha rightly put "What we are, is as a result of the thoughts we had". Thus, put your thoughts in a good direction. The matter which attracts attention is how far we are successful in driving and focusing our thoughts. Thoughts without right direction and focus would end no where. It would be like drawing lines on water or painting an ice cube.

Bharath always thinks about helping others, and he always advises his wife as well as friends about the same. They will definitely place him high for his lofty thoughts. But unless he transforms his thoughts into reality, he is a failure, and will never be admired. A very good example is Dr. A.P.J. Abdul Kalam, former President of India. He dreamt about a wonderful India in the course of the next 20 years, and he worked hard to achieve his goal. If you do not have good thoughts, you will not meet success. The thought process will be influenced by many factors like one's own **Beliefs**, **Attitudes** and **Values**. The thoughts put forward by our Father of the Nation were realized, when Indians were free from the hands of British.

In your personal life as well as professional life, you need to learn to impart good thoughts. In your personal life, you will think of studying well to score more marks and to win scholarships as a student. Your areas of concern will be getting up early in the morning, studying and preparing for exams, going to schools or colleges, meeting friends, playing with them, may be with a little joy and naughtiness. You will not be in an insecure position, because you have your parents or guardians to protect you. You will feel no sufferings. You will be entrusted the duties regarding studies only. You will also be engaged in joyous activities like tours, trekking etc, where you will really feel free of all the tensions and worries.

We always dream of going back to our school days again, where we enjoyed all sorts of above stated things, because when we enter our professional life, we will be standing entirely opposite to the position where we were standing in our school days. There we evaluate ourselves with the help of teachers, parents and friends etc. but in our professional life, we have to analyze, evaluate and develop ourselves. We may or may not get help from others. Here comes the need of self evaluation. Once we learn to evaluate ourselves, we will start developing.

How thoughts drive us to success

Thoughts are the driving force of our actions. Thus, we have to mould our thoughts to get optimum result. Our thoughts may be dependent on many factors like, one's own feelings, emotions, passion, beliefs, values, perception levels etc. The background of one's environment and circumstances will influence his thoughts too. To get good thoughts, one needs to be in the company of good people and good circumstances.

At this spot, a story comes to my mind. There was a lord ruling a territory. Next to his palace, there was a butcher. Each one of them possessed a parrot. The lord's parrot always spoke only good words, because it was used to good words only. Just opposite to it, the butcher's parrot spoke only filthy words, because it was used to filthy words from the butcher and his family. One day the butcher came to the lord and told him that his own parrot has turned to be a filthy creature, saying only bad words, and day by day it was getting worse. It was calling the wayfarers bad words. The butcher said in desperation that if it continued like this he might either kill the parrot, or do something else with it. The butcher was very sad with his parrot.

When the lord heard this matter, he suggested a way to reform the butcher's parrot. He let his royal parrot to be with the butcher's parrot so that it will learn at least good words from the royal parrot. Soon after a week, the butcher ran towards the lord again, and the lord was happy assuming that the royal parrot might have reformed the butcher's parrot so soon. He gave an ear to the butcher's words. But the butcher was so sad that he was about to cry. The lord was curious and asked the butcher to explain the matter. The butcher was really sad to explain the matter to the lord. But at last, he took the royal parrot and presented to the lord. As soon as the parrot was out of the cage, it started raining bad words at the lord first. The lord was embarrassed with the situation and was totally confused at the scene.

At that time the chief minister came to the scene and explained to the lord that the reverse thing had happened here. The royal parrot learned bad words from the butcher's parrot instead of the butcher's parrot learning good words from the royal parrot, What we need to learn is never indulge in bad company. If you do so you will get corrupted with bad people's influence.

Here we must learn one important thing that, **negative multiplies double and positive, half**. Thus, only when we realize ourselves, do we meet success. We need not give room for somebody to enter our good self and turn us bad. Instead we must try to impart good things to others. We need to transfer our knowledge and skills for the well being of others. As in the case of successful persons, you need be helping others to get salvation. Now a days, we come across many teenagers (usually called as problem agers), who really are bothersome. They lack respect to their parents, adults as well as teachers. They roam around simply without being responsible and at times turn to be antisocial elements. What we come across at this particular time would be their association with bad friends and bad circumstances. They tend to be like this only due to these factors. If they are implanted in a good atmosphere, they would definitely change.

The main reason why they act and behave this way is due to their hormonal changes. Generally, children below the age 12 are considered as common, without specific gender identities. That means, girls and boys behave and look similar. But, after age 12, hormonal changes bring about changes in boys and girls differently. These changes discriminate them as a boy or a girl. Those girls who were so active and extroverts might turn silent. This is due to the manifestation of their feminine qualities induced by female hormones. But, in the case of boys, the dominance of male hormones makes the difference. They would feel that some energy is being imparted into them, via the action of male hormones. They feel that some energy boosters or inducers have filled inside them. If these types of predispositions get sufficient opportunity through negative accommodations as stated above, they would definitely fall in to deep wells of problems and many psychological problems as a consequence.

Also, if they are put along with good people, they have fewer tendencies to change towards positive direction. This is what is explicitly clear in every human instinct for affinity towards negatives. Thus, a sincere advice to my adult readers, that, you should take extra care in rearing your teen age children. Also, sincere suggestions to my teen readers to be extremely aware of your problem age, and act accordingly. Do remember it is very easy to get bad names and remarks, but equally difficult to acquire good names and remarks. Thus, by understanding these basic facts, you need to live and let live accordingly, by never letting bad company grab you.

In personal as well as in official life, there are people who meet success to a great extent. We often meet such kind of people in various walks of life. Those who have succeeded in both personal as well as official life are the real winners. There are certain people who win in business life or official life, but, fail in personal life, and vice versa. Neither should happen. You need to be an overall winner, to balance various life situations.

Those who exclusively concentrate in business or pure official matters, don't have enough time to concentrate in their family matters. Thus their family feels upset and dejected and slowly might result in the collapse of families. The increasing number of divorces and many other family related issues originate from this basic issue.

I came across a case in my clinic, wherein a husband and wife got into lots of conflicts and accusations. Initially they were accusing each other to the core. Both are working IT professionals. They were having severe night schedules as well. Both had rare direct meeting occasions. When one came home after work, the other had to go out to work. They didn't have adequate time to spend together, in the mad pursuit of gaining money and position / career. In the discussion, they did not even remember when they last had sex. Thus, the problems were many. I understood they lacked enough time to share for each other. Instead, they were running for only material life at the loss of their very personal life. They earned in terms of money, but nothing in terms of their own life.

I suggested to them to take a few days' break from their schedules and try living together for each other. A few months later I got a call from them letting me know the good news that they were going to be father and mother. They were really thankful to me for guiding them to effective life. They came to understand their areas of development, and now they live for each other as well.

See what happened to their lives. A small tuning made their lives entirely different. This type of awareness about our own lives can make sufficient turning points in our lives. Make each and every second of your life enjoyable moments, and live it to the core.

When one doesn't get ample time to be with his beloved, he will ultimately end up in desperation. He might lose his beloved and loneliness becomes his friend. I advise you to give due care and consideration to those who are important to you. Amidst whatever issues or work related activities, you should not forget about your family. They are your assets. Your parents, wife and children, everyone accumulate to form the complete "you". Otherwise you will be incomplete.

Give your valuable time to all those significant to you. That means you are giving some part of your life to them, because, time is your life. If a part of your life in the form of some time is given to your beloved, see the difference in your life. Personal grudges would dissolve and you will feel the new way of life coming to you with a new fragrance and dew drops will shower upon your life in the form of happiness and creativity.

There is a story regarding human value. This is about a father and a son. The father was a very busy person, and had to be away from home on business matters. The son loved his father very much. Once, after a long day's work and tension the father reached his home. On his arrival, the son was standing at the door. The son asked his father whether he was busy and he replied that he was not. Then the boy asked him how much money he made per hour. The father was so angry and told his son that he didn't have any time to waste with all sorts of childish talks like that. Also a small child like him need not know about such serious matters. Still the boy kept on asking the same question; at last the father told that per hour he was earning Rs. 100/-. Then the boy asked his father whether he could borrow Rs.50/- from him. The father was so furious and told the boy that it was none of his business to know how much he was earning or things of that sort. He ordered the boy to go to bed.

The infuriated father began to think about his son's question. At first he thought that his son was asking money for the purchase of some unnecessary toys or gifts. But soon he calmed down and put himself in the boy's position. May be he asked money for some other matter, and he went to his son's bedroom.

The father asked him why he wanted Rs. 50/-. The boy didn't say anything. After that the father gave him the money. The boy was delighted and he picked up some money from under his pillow and counted Rs. 50. Thus the boy had a total of Rs.100/- with him. The father became agitated and asked the boy why he asked money again if he had some already with him.

Then the boy gave the whole amount to his father and asked whether he could buy an hour from him. The furious father cooled down and hugged his son and consoled him. He understood his fault and thereafter acted sensibly. He found time to spend with his son however busy he was.

Most of us are like him. We don't find time to be with our family. We usually roam around for something else. The real treasure of love and comfort lies with our family. By not understanding it, we run behind money or power. We need to show our value by pleasing those who rely upon us first. What you get is what you give. If you don't give something to your people, after a period of time you will be a stranger in front of your grown up children. They might not be intimate with you, as they see you very rarely and you don't get ample time to love them.

There was a very eye wetting situation where one of my friends' father expired. Almost all his children were settled abroad. Two of them were at that time present for the cremation ceremonies as per Indian custom. One of his sons was in the USA. His wife had received employment around that time, and they were unable to come home to pay the last rites for the departed father. They couldn't come home to see their mother even after months. This was definitely due to their busy schedule, but, of course they failed to be a part of the family at a very critical moment. Let us put our thoughts together and think about our parents who spent their lives for us, and nurtured and cared for us. At least there should be some commitment on our part to take care of them. It is the duty of all children. Let us pray for them for a while on this occasion.

I am the eldest son of my elderly parents, a 71 year old mother and 81 year old father. In my thirties, you see, I was quite unable to move about looking after my own family and business. Even though I got highly lucrative openings outside my place, I denied everything, because, I believe that my gain is the prayers of my parents, which will protect me for ever. I carry such a different thought, but I don't know how many of my readers would agree to my view. I am sure it is only because of their blessings and love that I have become a writer and you have come to know about me. Otherwise, I would also be roaming here and there, at the cost of my own love and affection. Tomorrow, my son also has to look after me in my old age. As the very proverb states, "What you sow is what you reap". Only if you look after your parents today, will your children do the same to you. So, please bear in mind not to dump your parents in the old age homes that are booming these days. If you have any plan of doing that, think of yourselves in the same position later.

Specialty of Love and Respect

The unique thing about love and respect is that only if you give them will you get them back. There are some people who claim love and respect. These guys won't know the uniqueness of these two delicate feelings, love and respect. As already told regarding Newton's law, what you give alone will you get. This is very strong regarding love and respect.

There is a saying that instead of helping a human if you give a bit of bread to a dog, it will really love you and see you as his master. But, different is the case with human beings. They really will hesitate to show gratitude in return.

Already all of us would be really familiar with this common human nature.

There was a husband and wife. They were really happy and enjoyed their life really like anything when they were newly married. But after a couple of years there was a gap between them. The husband complained that his wife didn't love him, and the wife also expressed the same concern. There was a strong issue and it turned very serious as well.

They approached me once, for counseling. After a detailed discussion with them, I found out that there was no problem between them and that was the problem. But the husband was a bit selfish. He only demanded love or claimed it, and never gave it back. Same is his case with others. He always complained about her family. What he told was that nobody from her family respected him. Was the complaint a genuine one? I don't think so. If he feels that nobody respects him, I would say it's his mistake. He might not know the basic principle of love and respect.

So friends, take it from me. Unless you understand the real value of love and respect, you will reach nowhere. The above stated story throws light to the same fact.

The relevance of consideration

Consideration is a significant thing which is very sensitive and need to be taken care with due importance. It is linked to love and respect, or else we can call as a blend of both. The more we consider, the more will we also be considered. The very term consideration has many dimensions for our understanding. We need to consider anything and everything that is found important.

It is difficult to find out which is relevant and which is not. That is why it is called "sensitive". We have been endowed with some extraordinary gifts from god like common sense and discretionary power. We have to make use of them to sort out what is good and what is bad. Especially this is important in human relationships. It is like a glass. A small crack would make it useless. Thus beware. Relationships are really very sensitive and have to be specially taken care of. Thus, give consideration to each and everyone associated with you. No doubt, they will one day consider you as well.

Chapter 5

Thought Parameters

We will now discuss about thoughts a little bit. As we have seen, thoughts are very important and each and every deed you perform is purely based on them. For a person to be good within, one needs to reform from within and should be extraordinarily perfect in many areas. As discussed earlier, everything starts from thoughts. Thus, for good thoughts to generate within, you need to focus on certain things to be developed within you. The following are the areas we need to give attention to:

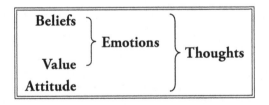

The basic attributes contributing to thoughts will be one's Beliefs, Values and Attitudes. Beliefs and Values contribute to one's Emotions. Thus, Emotions and Attitude nurture one's thoughts, or Thought is a function of Beliefs, Values and Attitudes. Let us analyze each segment in detail.

Beliefs

Beliefs play an important role in moulding a personality. It is only belief that makes and breaks ones personality. It is resultant from one's place of birth to the current position. A major part is played by the environment and the situations from where one has come. Childhood is really an important influencing factor. The circumstances in which one is being brought up really matters. It is very important for one's personality. Thus one's beliefs play a vital role in building his thoughts.

One with good beliefs can definitely build good thoughts. We will discuss the 'belief' part in great detail so that we can make ourselves fit to build good thoughts.

Beliefs may take many forms like:

- Self belief / belief in one's own self
  - o Knowledge
    - Internal
    - External
    - Skill
  - o Courage
  - o Mutual Belief
  - o Belief in friends / colleagues
  - o Family members
  - o organization
- Belief in God/Religion

Let's discuss one by one in detail.

Self belief / belief in one's own self

This could otherwise be called as self confidence / belief, i.e. belief in one's own self. For a person to believe in himself, he needs to have a clear idea about himself. For that the main parameters would be having a thorough study of oneself. All the successful persons we see around us believe in themselves. Some examples are Mahatma Gandhi, Sardar Vallabh Bhai Patel, Raja Ram Mohan Roy etc.

In the present scenario, Dhirubhai Ambani, Ratan Tata, Birla etc. come to our mind. If we have self confidence, we will reach the level we desire. There are no simple ways to achieve it. It can be achieved only through a thorough self-study. All of us have heard about the legend, the great Bruce Lee. Even after years of his demise, we do remember him. It was due to the impact he made in our minds.

To tell about his life, he started his career as a waiter in some restaurant in China. After his work hours, he attended Kung Fu classes and practiced hard. It was nothing but his self-confidence that raised him up to the desired level. He turned to be a legend. He would be the first one from the east to be a superstar in Hollywood. The determination and confidence expressed by him was immense.

Regarding his physique, he was a lean and short fellow in his younger days. In those days he exhibited immense body flexibility and expertise in martial arts. He then started weight training to build his body. Thus he improved his health and became stronger to win tournaments. He wanted to make himself known to the world. His self confidence and determination had driven him to success.

The example set by Bruce Lee reminds us that it is not only one's physical appearance or looks that make one touch success, but one's self confidence. Each and everyone among us will be able to meet success if we have the real thrive for that.

When we speak about this, the picture of a spider that weaves a web to catch prey comes to our mind. It would take hours to weave a single thread of a web. Even if it breaks once, the spider tries its level best till the task is achieved; otherwise, it would die of hunger. Thus, if someone wants to live, he must do the tasks or occupations entrusted upon them. Like this, we have many other lessons from nature which could make us think and look in to ourselves and grow.

To support one's confidence, the following things will definitely help.

Knowledge

Knowledge can be information, facts, data, acquaintance, familiarity, awareness, understanding, comprehension etc. literally. We need to be basically aware of many things, like those inevitable for our work as well as life. There are many ways of acquiring knowledge. It comes from many sources too. But one has to be ready for acquiring knowledge. He has to keep his eyes and ears open to the world, and should have a sense of direction. Only with a drive for acquiring knowledge, will you gain it. What I mean to say is that, only if you have the real thirst to acquire knowledge, will you get it, and can make use of it.

If we feel thirsty, we will at any cost go in search of water to satisfy it. If we don't have that feeling of thirst, we will not search for water. If we drink it, we feel really satisfied. But, there is a small difference in the case of knowledge thirst. It should not get satiated, and should go on and on for ever, till the end of one's life. Thus, the thirst for knowledge should be unquenchable.

Those with a real thirst for knowledge alone will survive in the long run, among geniuses. You need to be outstanding, not standing out. In the knowledge arena, you need to be thirsty to acquire maximum knowledge.

There are two variants of knowledge like Internal Knowledge and External Knowledge.

Internal Knowledge

While telling about knowledge, first of all we need to be aware of ourselves. That is called as self knowledge or here internal knowledge. Thus internal knowledge is one's own measurement about him/her. What are my strengths? What are my weaknesses? You need to ask similar questions to yourself and answer them yourself.

First of all you need to be aware of your weaknesses rather than your strengths. Then only will you be able to draw the line of limit pertaining to yourself. Unless you do that, there will not at all be a control to the extent that you can perform. It may go out of control. This can be substantiated with a simple example.

There was a person called Babu who was a swimmer. He could swim in the sea, pond, lake or river. He was highly confident of his swimming skills and was ready to take any challenge on that. When one asked him the distance he could swim, he easily replied that he could swim for 2000 meters continuously. The interesting thing was that he was really that confident of himself and he assumed to be a great swimmer.

With this limited swimming skills he went to swim and cross the English Channel which is so wide; to swim across it would be almost equivalent to committing suicide. But he was so daring that he faced death by simply welcoming it. We should never be over confident. If we are, we may end up in despair.

Thus, before knowing our strengths, we need to know our weaknesses. Thus, internal knowledge would be a measurement of one's weaknesses and strengths. If you are strong on certain areas, you need to nourish those and make them grow and flourish. There are people who are good at selling, accounting, engineering skills etc. They need to recognize these skills and make them grow instead of ending up in problems. Instead of recognizing what we can, we go on doing something else which actually cannot be done by us, and we reach nowhere. Thus, my sincere suggestion to my friends, never end up in failures. Always gain successes through thorough self evaluation.

Many parents have been found to compel their children to choose their careers. Some of them would not like the sort of career paths shown by their parents, and they have a different outlook. But, by not understanding the real strengths of their children, parents compel their children to choose something else, which might be out of reach by them actually. They would first of all do the work imposed upon them without any interest or willingness. They may fail however much they try for it, as they do it without self confidence or real interest. My sincere suggestion to parents is, not to compel your children, and let them choose the subjects in which they have real interest.

Innate Strengths

Strength can be of many types. It may also take many forms depending on certain situations and circumstances. There are some people who don't talk unnecessarily or indulge in activities which are out of their reach or interest. They seem to be silent and calm. But at times they would burst out of the limits to the entire surprise of others. This type of strength is called as innate or in built strength, about which they are really not aware of. We might at times come across certain silent people, who, on a fine morning become owners of a business or are posted on a responsible job and they are found to perform well. This is due to their innate strengths hidden in them, and unknown to them and others, and manifest in many forms, when they get an opportunity to express it.

Innate strengths will be like one's own in built or inherent strengths. It is in their genetic make up. If they are found out and developed, they would reach anywhere. But what happens in many cases will be lack of proper identification or at times recognition of the same. As we discussed earlier, if the real interest is not found and developed, one might not perform, and can take a reverse turn as well. Thus, we come to understand that one needs to be working within the frame work of one's real interest, and shine. If one is put in to other areas out of one's interests, one will underperform.

Acquired Strengths

There are certain cases where people have acquired mental and physical strengths from their experiences. They might have gone through terrible extremes of mental or physical pressures or strains, and as a result, might have got adjusted to all types of extreme conditions, through adaptation. The one main speciality and uniqueness of human body and brain is that, the more we use them, the more they develop. For example, if we use our biceps muscles, they will become bigger and gain strength. In the theory of evolution there is a statement that the biceps of a blacksmith would be more strong and developed comparatively. This would be due to the increased use of that particular muscle. Similarly, cart pullers have strong calf muscles, developed through continuous use. The case of our brain is not different. If we engage it in various ways, it gets sharper and can reach the level of excellence over a period of time.

Keep in mind to maintain good health. There are people around us who do tremendous hard work physically, but are under-healthy. It's due to improper nutrition necessary for the maintenance and repair of body, and anabolism. The strenuous physical activities demand sufficient nourishment for the body which is deprived. Thus, the output exceeds the input and the physique becomes under-healthy. The strain and stress put up is not compensated to the mark. Also, if we don't nourish the brain, it will under perform.

As a solution for this problem, the hard working ones need to be provided with sufficient nourishment or else they will end up in serious problems both physical and mental.

As discussed earlier, a healthy body develops the brain also. Thus, even if you are not that intelligent, you can to a certain limit reach the required level by putting your brain under healthy exercise. It may be like reading, writing, thinking, talking, listening to music, playing chess, caroms, puzzles, su-do-ku etc. The brain cells are to be developed to the required level. Sufficient level of aerobics or air taking activities also help support the healthy condition of physique as well as brain. Do you know the major part of the oxygen inhaled is consumed by the brain? It would come to around 70 to 80 percentage. Thus the brain would remain healthy when we supply sufficient oxygen to the brain. Thus, for a healthy body and brain give them proper nourishment as required. Only then will they work properly.

Next time, if you feel bored or depressed, make a short walk, stretch or just stand and sit on your chair so that the heart beat increases and more oxygen is taken in which is beneficial for the whole body. All the physical as well as mental activities will be enhanced to the required levels. It would be just as if the air-cooled engine is made to cool by using cooling fins as in the case of motor-cycles, and water radiators in the case of heavy vehicles. The more air you take in, the more it can enhance the activity of your body and brain. It is also another way of nourishment.

All of us are born with no special sort of skills. All that we possess are acquired. There are indeed certain things which are inherent, like the figure and physique, the general thoughts, the basic body language, the basic speech style etc. But what is important is the level of exposure to various conditions in life like surroundings, environment, culture, customs etc. to which one might be exposed. All the factors gained through such exposures are called as acquired ones, and those within, as inherent ones.

There are certain people who have tremendous inherent or in-built qualities like analytical skills, reasoning ability, basic / general intelligence, high Intelligent Quotient (IQ) etc. They excel in academic activities, studies etc. and they touch heights too. Now a days they are into software development and related IT sector. The people with such innate skills shall be made stronger through thorough stringent induction programs and can perform better at work especially, provided they have the right attitude.

The other segment of people with average types of above stated skills can achieve development with thorough and stringent induction for a required period. They can be developed to a certain extent.

There are another set of people with very low levels of the required sets of qualities, which through even stringent and strict inductions and trainings could not be developed. Their IQ and related capacities are very low.

There are also some classes of people who, in spite of having sufficient stated qualities, will not work or put their brain into anything. They simply roam around without doing anything. If they put themselves into some productive areas, they will be able to develop much. But right attitude is lacking in them. We will discuss about attitudes later.

External Knowledge

External knowledge, as told earlier, is an acquired type of knowledge. This brings a great impact upon our lives. What we see, hear, feel, smell and taste adds to our knowledge base and forms the external or acquired knowledge. We are reminded of Pavlov's motivational theory and his experiment explaining behavior. A dog was kept under captivity and offered food every time after ringing a bell. It was made a routine for a certain period of time. The dog was used to the ringing of bell just before its food was delivered. Soon after, in the process of experiment, after the bell ringing the food was not delivered. When tested, the dog was found to be salivating as if it was getting ready to have food. The previous process of bell ringing accompanied by food was recorded in its brain. Whenever it heard the bell, it was reminded of the forthcoming food just after that. Thus it salivated automatically, expecting the food. This similar process of conditioned learning occurs to us as well at times.

Through this process, the dog learned that whenever the bell rang its food was about to come and its brain gave appropriate signals to discharge saliva. It happened without the knowledge of the dog. It was taken care of by the brain and concerned hormonal activities.

Learning through Experiences

All the learning processes are similar. We learn things from our experiences. Majority of our knowledge is of acquired type. It is through all our sense organs. It may be through ears, eyes, nose, tongue or skin. If we see a beautiful object, it gets recorded in a special area of the brain, and as it is an interesting thing, we recall it when the recorded image comes from our brain to memory. It comes back to our memory whenever the occasion demands.

If we see an ugly object, it will also be recorded and retrieved as said earlier, but not with pleasant mood as of earlier. If we stepped on mud or cow dung, always we will be reminded by our brain of being cautious about the mud or dung and not to step on it again. Such processes are called **"Response to Stimulus"**.

To give another example, if we are pricked by a thorn while plucking a rose flower and starts bleeding, next time definitely we will be cautious. From the previous incident what we learn is that whenever we pluck a rose flower, we need to be cautious otherwise we may be hurt.

For such a thing to happen there has to be a stimulus initially. In our example, the stimulus is the thorn pricking us and the response will be pulling back our hands. Those are the successful ones who learn from each and every experience in their lives. Those who do so will succeed and others will fail. Thus stimuli are coaches who teach us about external situations.

There are many situations which are positive while many are negative ones. Through positive things we learn more. But through negative ones we learn a lot more, **because the experiences are not better but bitter**. Thus, response to stimulus would contribute a bulk volume to our experiences. Learning through experiences also creates a real impact in our lives, which we would never forget. It is also the same as external knowledge.

Life's tough

It's clearly stated that life is really a threat to all. To survive is a challenge, to cope up with the uncertainties too complex; to withstand the storm, tough and to keep the pace is difficult. Thus each and every one of us need to be really active to keep the pace of life, be really strong to tolerate the tough situations, be predictable to cope up with the uncertainties, and be bold to face the challenges.

There are some people around us who never view life with its required seriousness. They play with it, damage it, try to repair, and at last end up in despair. The value of life and living it in its full tempo doesn't mean anything to them. To live a life so normal or by leaving it to itself is very comfortable. To live it as per our rule and with full satisfaction will look too difficult.

We usually find people inside trains in the form of beggars, handicapped people etc. who usually come before us singing songs, dancing and doing acrobatics etc. There are also some who earn money by cleaning the compartments dirtied by passengers.

Apart from all these, there are also vendors who sell hot coffee, milk or cool water or soft drinks. I imagine myself doing all these and feel terrified. Neither the hot coffee nor the cold milk or water entertains me. I buy all these that appear before me so as to support those who sell them.

There are incidents where I used to give beggars some penny too.

While discussing all these matters, I remember some people who waste their time sitting upon the platforms of shops, bus stations etc. simply wasting their time. They never wish to do anything but simply blame those who work hard. Even if you give some work to them they won't do it. Those class of people could be called national wastes or good for nothing fellows.

Skill

So far we have discussed some relevant snapshots regarding an important part of self-belief, that is, knowledge. Now let me attempt to put some light on skills. Literally, skill is ability, talent, cleverness, dexterity, expertise, proficiency, deftness, handiness and so on. How can our skills help us gain success and how can each one of us identify our specific skills? Skills can be called as applied knowledge. The skills and knowledge are at times interrelated. If knowledge is applied in a right sense, skills are formed. For example, we learn about teaching skills. After acquiring the needed knowledge regarding the subject, we put it in to action, thereby transforming the knowledge in to action in the form of skills, here, via teaching. If we have good knowledge, we can apply it as good skills and vice versa. I request the readers to relate this with the "knowledge" session. Skills are similar to knowledge in the sense that they also are **innate** and **acquired**. There are some types of skills which are transferable as well.

Innate Skills

These are the sorts of skills which are inborn or genetic or hereditary. They may be unique to a single person. Some examples are learning skills, fast running skills, withstanding / tolerance skills etc. Some people are fast learners. They can grasp things very fast. This is an extraordinary skill. Similarly, some people will have tremendous innate stamina to withstand physical stress and strain. Others may have to try so hard to achieve the same. These types of skills are usually called as innate skills. Thus, innate skills could be called as those prototyped in to one's personality, by virtue of his or her genetic constitution.

You might have noticed some people with a good body shape naturally and we call them natural structure or figure. These types of physical structures may be called natural ones, which are obtained by them naturally.

We might have seen experts in many fields. They perform certain tasks very easily which might be very difficult for others to even try. Some make tasty food, some repair things so easily, some teach very easily, some drive vehicles so fast without any fear. These are all examples of innate strengths / skills.

Acquired Skills

These are the skills which are acquired from experiences or training. Some people will try so hard to achieve things. Runners and athletes try and get trained so hard to meet success. Some try hard in studies. These are called acquired skills. The new things which we learn through our wish and will can be called acquired skills.

As stated above, some have to really try to achieve a good physical appearance through vigorous physical exercises.The skills like trekking, jumping, running etc. could be achieved through thorough physical training.

Let us now discuss how one's skills could help him build his own belief and good thoughts. Skills help one to apply one's knowledge to a relevant area. A skilled person is extra self confident, and as discussed earlier, will in turn be able to build good thoughts, thereby creating good skills and better work performance.

Courage

For one to build his self belief or confidence, one needs to be courageous. However skilled he is, unless he possesses a certain level of courage, he never will be able to excel in his field, be it complex or simple. Just for an example, one person may be inducted with knowledge to a great extent, but may lack sufficient courage so that his training or presentation skills have no value. Thus, to build courage within oneself is an inevitable factor for one's success.

To build courage doesn't mean to acquire immense volumes of it and be rude to everybody. It will create a negative impact only. You need to acquire an optimum level of it for your success. There are people around us who may be not talkative, or seem to be a bit shy. But they might be successful in their life. They might possess the required level of courage to excel in their field. When we hear about courage, we suddenly think of violence, of attacking somebody, which is not true. It has to be redirected in a focused manner so as to create good result. Otherwise, it will also be a problem.

Every day we read, see and hear about violence, killing, hitting, burning etc, which are the impact of negative effects of courage, when people use the same in a negative sense. There are also some people who excel in business, do jobs, study well and perform well in many other means. All these are the results of the positive impact of courage. We are the ones to make the choice, whether to use it positively or negatively. My dear readers, awake, and use your courage in a productive manner, so that, it will affect you and your society in a positive manner, and vice versa.

If a person possesses adequate levels of courage, then only can he apply his knowledge and skills at relevant areas. Even though he possesses enough knowledge and skill, if he is hesitant or reluctant to apply it, he will be a real failure in life. He needs to possess enough courage to refine his knowledge and skills which will lead to build his thoughts in a positive manner.

Mutual Belief

To live a good and exceptional life, one needs to be ready to build good interpersonal relationships. It is a very reflecting factor in one's life. Unless you own excellent interpersonal relations, you will not at all be able to touch heights. To build good interpersonal relationships is not easy, but not that tough as well. Mutual belief is one's belief upon others. The 'others' may be persons or organizations. It has different variants as per the situations.

Relationships have mutual expectations (Relationships are Materialistic)

Everything on earth runs basically on mutual belief. A mother believes in children that they would take care of her at her old age, and takes care of them. Same way, children believe in parents thinking that they would take care of them as well. Teachers believe that their children would improve and children believe that, teachers would take care of them. Similar is the case with husband-wife, lovers, friends etc. If you do something to someone, your mind will look for some gratification, in some forms. It takes the form of some returns, may be in the form of money, materials or services. It can be help as well. A son loves his mother for the services she provides which serve his gratification of needs. For example, the kid is very much attached to his mother expecting mother's milk, and later when he is a bit older, for the food his mother provides. Like wise, he is attached to his parents in return for love, praise, food, shelter etc. Also, parents take care of their children, expecting their children to take care of them in future, when they are old.

Now a days, parents put extra efforts in the studies of their children. Some wish to make them some professionals as they plan, without considering the interests of the children, expecting that, if they are made so, their needs can be gratified, and can stand before the society with utmost pride. It is none other than this subconscious satiation of needs that make them do such things, instead of true love and affection towards their children.

Some incidents like approval and affection towards select employees doesn't make much difference. Such recognitions and special love are manifestations of the Boss' expectations from such employees, something special and extra, in the form of results or profit, when compared to other employees. Such instances prove that everything in life is materialistic.

Belief in friends

All of us will be very much aware of the saying, 'A friend in need is a friend indeed'. This is the value of friendship. The real value of friendship cannot be measured or predicted. There is a very famous proverb regarding friendship which states **"Friendship is not the collection of hearts, but**

selection of hearts. "Fine friends open my eyes, smart friends open my mind, but only sweet friends open my heart". This is another statement of different kinds of friends. There are depictions for friendship in various epics as well.

There are some friends who are really our real and true guides, who open our eyes, through their fantastic deeds. They provide us the dos and don'ts in different situations. At times they could be made models as well, in our day to day life.

Some classes of friends are very energetic and smart. They do everything very well and things are much better with them. Things will be much safer with them too. They can be called as **smart friends**.

Another class of friends is **sweet ones**. They will be very sweet by nature. They will be as delicate as ice cream. They can never be shattered at any cost. They steal everybody's heart. They will be so nice to be handled. They will be very light at mind. Generally girl friends come under this class. Seldom are some boys as sweet as them. They will never create any sort of problems to anybody.

Next class of friends are the rude ones, like **rough and tough**. They will never mingle with anyone, till the same frequency is met with. They are the class of generally problematic ones. They gang together to do filthy deeds. They are the classes that cannot be trusted. They lack qualities. They might be kept separate. They would fall under antisocial personality types at times.

Thus select a good heart as your friend and don't collect many hearts unnecessarily. It might cause very serious problems. A trusted friend can give you much. Thus belief in your friend will be an added advantage for you. To have trustworthy friends, selection must be done very wisely. You can really put your problems before a good friend, and he can really help you out in solving any problem.

To get such a true friend is very difficult. It may take much time to get one like that. But once you are through, you are very lucky with that matter. A friend of such type can be anyone or anybody. It can be your father, mother, brother, sister, spouse, classmate, colleague etc. It may vary from person to person and situation to situation.

There are many instances where all of the above stated can be one's friend. But, a friend in your whole life, as stated earlier to be available is very difficult. It's a matter of luck too. You can get a wife or husband in your life. But to get a spouse as your lifetime friend, it's too difficult. If you are able to, then you are really lucky.

Belief in colleagues

Who are colleagues? Are they our friends? Or are they our co-workers? Are they our classmates? Or are they something else? It is better to define them as co-workers or team mates. To explain this better would be to take some snapshots from our lives. We might have many colleagues, those from our present organization and many more from our previous organizations.

As we are with our colleagues during the major part of the day, we need to have a very strong rapport with them, so that the situations will be smooth. Our work atmosphere will be made more enjoyable. As the modern work system mainly relies upon mutual belief, the belief in our colleagues plays a major role in our work situations. It doesn't mean that you alone should keep believing others every time and not get back the same belief from others. Organizations have to put their vision in such direction for mutual belief.

Colleagues occupy different levels from top to bottom in your department or team.Thus you need to be associated with all levels in the organizational hierarchy. The level of interaction differs from person to person or the levels in the hierarchy. It may be more with your co-workers or immediate team members, which might fall down to other department members and so on. Thus, to become more interactive with your colleagues, you need be associated with them more, depending on the levels. I have encountered many, who act like Bosses in an organization. They always address themselves as "Boss" only, and always try to make others subservient to them. But, friends, is this possible now a days? I have my own doubts. Modern management doesn't demand such useless people called as Bosses in the system, but rather it needs "Leaders", to be more precise.

There are innumerable differences between a "Leader" and a "Boss", of which some relevant ones are given here for your understanding.

Boss	**Leader**
Drives his men	Inspires his team
Depends on Authority	Depends on Goodwill
Evokes Fear	Radiates Love
Says "I"	Says "We"
Shows who is wrong	Shows how to do it
Abuses men	Uses men
Demands Respect	Commands Respect
Makes work Drudgery	Makes work joyful

After going through these, we are the ones to choose what we need to become. I request my readers to be very sensible to make the right choice which is demanding to your environment and area of operation. There are lots of cases wherein we see lots of employee attrition happens now days. The employees are leaving the organizations so rapidly due to lack of satisfaction, or when running short of their satisfaction needs. They might be earning good salaries; even then they leave, due to lack of satisfaction in their jobs. A major catalyst in the same issue is a 'people problem' like "Bosses' issues".

People always complain that they are unable to "adjust" to the job environment. What does it mean? The environment just means people. To our wonder, the biggest problems we face in our lives are "People Problems", which is very difficult to resolve. But, it is resolved, the biggest problem in the society remains unresolved. It is better to resolve it by ourselves. There are no special techniques to resolve this issue, as it is related to people. The people problem has to be resolved by people themselves, i.e. us. Each and every one of us needs to be extra conscious of this issue, that, the major setback we face among people are problems related to people.

We know that some people are afraid of dead bodies, and they hesitate to see a dead body or stand beside it as well. Friends, to such people, I ask, why should we fear dead bodies, when live bodies are to be feared actually? My dear friends, thus, looking from this angle, do we make any difference between us and animals? It is a very serious thought we need to dwell upon. Actually, this comparison itself doesn't have any value, because, we human beings are said to have increased mental ability comparatively, and we live in the frame work of certain rules and regulations, which, animals lack. Thus, even in spite of all these, we behave unusually, and poor animals, without having such frame work behave in their own way, which at times seems to be comparatively better than that of human beings. If animals have such rules and regulations, I think, of course they would behave far better than us, the most intelligent and able beings on Earth.

We were discussing about various human relationships, emphasizing upon colleagues. There are many types of colleagues that we encounter on a periodic basis. They may vary from very friendly through friendly, to rough and unfriendly. It all depends upon the situations and the environment generally. It could be very tough, tough, easy and very easy to act upon different situations. It all depends upon individual interests and capabilities to vary the frequency accordingly. Those who are experts in frequency modulation regarding the same would win and others lose. This type of frequency modulation in relationships with colleagues is called as official / job adjustment, or simply, getting attuned to job situations.

As discussed earlier, the major problem in our lives is "people" problem, and to resolve it is a skill called as "man management" skills. To be a good manager, you need to be well versed in man management skills, rather than materials management skills. To resolve man power related issues, the better equipment is manpower itself, in the form of proper management of the same. Unless it is done properly, the problem remains unresolved.

Thus, there should not be the term "Boss" in our system, and need to be replaced by "Leader", and we all choose to be only Leaders so as to survive in the system.

What I intend to bring before you is the need and importance of colleagues and how to deal with them. We usually encounter different types of people in our work environment. Here I don't wish to go more scientifically into the topic of different types of personalities, but to bring before you some common types of people we usually encounter. For example, there are people with ego. They may be called **egoistic** or **negative** ones. They never admit or recognize anybody. They are their own masters. They also will never allow others to go above them. They also pretend that they know everything. They don't like anybody else perform well and suppress others who shine more. They also never support others. They will be pure negative sort of characters. They will also be called as problem finders. Those who find problems in others can never sleep peacefully. For it to happen, first of all they themselves need to be fault free initially. Egoistic people usually never entertain or get entertained. They like to play "Boss" and get things done by any means, without sweating their body. Many a times such ones reach top level as well, by smashing down the performers, and enjoying the rewards actually meant to be enjoyed by the real performers. It is actually very difficult to manage and tackle such people. People will really fear to do something against them, because they tend to be dangerous as well. They will do anything to achieve their aim.

There are others in our work place who act superior. They are people with **superiority** complex. They never allow anybody to cross them. They are comparatively better than the first stated ones. They will be supportive to a certain extent. Even though they are negative, sometimes they are found to be supportive at times. Thus they might not be called pure negatives. They don't like to be led, but to lead. They have a tendency to get praised. If that's done, they are good ones. They will fall for it. They tend to know everything.

Another class of people possess **inferiority** complex. They always feel subordinate to others. Whenever they perform anything, they always worry how it will be interpreted by others. They are always skeptic about themselves as well as about others. They lack self confidence, and other positive personality traits. The main reason for them to be so may be numerous. They possess a very subtle self-image, i.e. they under-estimate themselves. It might also be due to many factors, like the environment in which they were brought up, genetic predisposition to be so etc. They usually lack leadership qualities, and tend to act exactly opposite to those of the superior types. They are also very difficult to manage. They will very rarely come up to the main stream unless proper training is provided to them. Psycho-therapies like Cognitive Behaviour Therapy and the like will do well for them. Individual counselling would rather add more to them than group counselling, which was my experience.

At times, such people will seem to show off or boast around in order to hide their inferiority complex. One incident which immediately comes to my memory is the case of a person, who wears only expensive apparels. Every time when someone presents him with medium priced ones, he is reluctant to wear the same. I noticed that those who gave him less expensive gifts did not have much money. When analyzed, it came to my notice that, the said person lacked a positive self-image. He found himself short, dark and feared people would not accept him the way he wanted. This type of inferiority complex built inside him reflected in many areas of his operations. He found his wife more beautiful than him, and always harassed her. He felt jealous when his wife interacted with her friends and family. I am unable to reveal his full story of complexes, because, it is never ending. Imagine how much his wife would have been struggling to get adjusted to such a person. At times, he behaves very decently as well, especially outside his family. This makes it difficult for his wife to expose his actual character to others, because he is very good outside, and no body would blame him on that matter.

Some others in our work place will have mixed sort of personality traits. Sometimes they may be found having positive traits in them but at other times, with certain amount of negatives too. They fall in between egoistic and superiors, egoistic and inferiors or any of the combinations. Managing people is a skill. The above given information will hopefully throw some light upon your understanding of various types of people, which will help you to use it in your specific systems.

Apart from them, we might encounter some with psychosis or with neurosis, who may require special attention. Some Psycho-therapies and Counsellings, clubbed with medicines will really help to resolve such issues.

Belief in relatives

Who are relatives? They are really our own family members. They are our kith and kin. They are inevitable for our life to a certain extent, in many cultural contexts. We possess relatives of different nature depending upon their importance or rather the importance we attribute to them. Among those who are the most important are our parents. Our father and mother are our creators and we pay due respect to them. Indian culture depicts Mother (*Matha*) first, then Father (*Pitha*), then only comes Guru (*Teacher*) and at last God (*Deva*).

It is the trust we have on them and the trust they have on us that make the bond of relation much stronger. We can come and go at any time in our house. This is due to the trust we have for each other. Thus, to make the bond stronger, we need to trust them to a particular level. It is thus so painful to see someone who blames their parents. My dear readers please keep in mind the strain and pain your parents have put in in order to bring you up. They have really sacrificed a major part of their lives for you. Especially teenagers have a tendency to disobey and ignore their parents by maintaining bad friendship and company. People of all ages also have been found to engage in filthy deeds. Thus, my sincere advice to you all is to pay due respect to your parents and elders, with the order of importance, and it will certainly pay for you later in your life.

I think, it is, relevant at this point of time, to discuss a very sensitive matter regarding whether **there is God or not**. Seemingly interesting, we might have encountered many human Gods or Living Gods among us. I don't mean saints who are the purest at heart. But I mean those who sell spirituality. They might take the form of "Walking Gods" or "Living Gods". They at times misuse spirituality as a means of smuggling and the like, to make money. Let us leave this and try to answer our question of existence of God. As discussed earlier, God is present in and around us, which we always miss to see due to our ego and lack of self identification. You love people. That is the best way of realising God. There is no short cut to know God than to love all the beings on Earth, by God. "Love all, Pray to God" means exactly the same. There are people who go to holy places daily and at the same time curse others. Some have bad thoughts in their minds even though they believe in and pray to God. The above given proverb becomes live when we impartially love others, without any expectations. This type of unbiased love creates inside us the purity at heart, which no one can even touch. No negative forces can attack you or even touch your purest form achieved through such give and take of pure love.

You might have to distinguish between this kind of love with material love and business love. We have discussed the relevance of material love and expectation elsewhere, which is quite inevitable in our lives, but it could not be called the end point of all. The application rests on how we discriminate between both. In every relationship, there is the vibration of love, i.e. God. But when the relationships turn only to pure materialistic ones, we will not be able to even think about God. There is yet another thought "God is Love". Thus it is up to us to decide upon our lives whether it should be with or without God.

The next level of relations are our brothers and (or) sisters. We grow with them, playing, chatting, quarrelling etc. We need to pay due love and concern towards them for successfully carrying out our lives in our family. We usually hear about the sparks arising in such relationships.

The reason for it could be mainly money or property. Interestingly enough, there are fewer chances for love as a cause. They don't quarrel for undertaking the responsibility of looking after their old parents, but only for their property. My dear readers please bear in mind, it is not money or property that is our ultimate goal, but it is pure love which encompasses everything. Before quarrelling for money, my dear brothers and sisters, please rewind your thoughts when you were growing together playing with each other in your childhood. Never break serene relationships of brotherly and sisterly nature for want of money or property. Also remember how painful it will be for the parents who see unhealthy problems crop up between their children. These might cause severe physical and mental problems to them as well. **It is easy to break one relation, but tough to make one**.

The next level of relationships are our uncles and aunts, sisters and brothers of our father and mother etc. Each and every person has different levels of attachment with different levels of relatives. For some, their uncles or aunts are more important than even their father and mother. It may be that they have been brought up by them due to many circumstances. It may differ from person to person, depending upon situations.

Thus, what we should bear in mind is that, each and every person important to us must be given due consideration and affection. The actions we perform might not be always similar. It may vary with people, time, situations, environment, circumstances etc. We have a good level of discretionary power to evaluate these and act wisely and skillfully to achieve maximum benefit and goodness in life.

But, always remember the very fact that relationship is like a glass. A simple scratch will spoil its quality. Thus beware while using this glass.

Belief in organization

By "organization" what I wish to present before you is the organization in which we work, or the same which we are associated with. It is really the group or the company which pays us for what we have done, or in simple terms our very soul and life. It gives us food, better opportunities, better scope for life, better work culture, better colleagues, better contacts and many more. Thus, to be in a good organization is to be into a good living. Thus, each one who works in an organization has to stick to the **Organizational Objectives,** i.e. the rules and regulations including the basic motto of business achievements. Remember, the organization is made up of small entities including each worker. It can be from a peon to Chairman. Everyone is equally responsible for the making and destroying of it. Unless each of us plays our roles appropriately, the organization cannot survive. Thus we are responsible for its construction and destruction. My sincere advice to all my readers, whatever position you may hold in an organization, is to play your roles well, and without trespassing in to someone else's jurisdiction. Never pull others' legs. First, focus on the entire Organizational Objectives, and then in to your specific objectives and do work accordingly. You will gain peace of mind along with money. Otherwise you will get only money and run short of peace of mind.

Each one of us pay due respect to the deeds we perform towards the organization and vice versa. The organization maintains us or rather retains us. We need to have the right sense of understanding and interest in it. The organization for which we work is our bread giver and to give the maximum from our side to it will be a pious deed from our side.

We all know the basic fact that only if there is a canvas can one draw pictures. Unless a suitable one is achieved, the artist never succeeds in portraying his ideas upon the canvas. Similar is the case with our organization too. If we do not have the organization (our business or profession), we will not be able to draw our life pictures i.e. we will not be able to meet our both ends together. Thus, it is our prime responsibility to maintain the canvas so as to enable us to draw numerous pictures. I would like to share a different thought with my readers. In our life, we need to marry twice, or in other words, we should have two wives. One reality is that, the second wife will stand with you only if the first wife is strong, or in other words, the second wife will come to your life only after seeing the credibility of your first wife. Confused, aren't you? Don't think otherwise. Let me break the confusion. By first wife, I mean our job / profession / business. The second wife of course is our real wife or spouse. Now just read those lines again and resolve the confusion. A real credible profession alone helps you maintain good family life, and nothing else.

The organization keeps a certain level of belief in us. It is only due to the same reason it retains us and pays us. The sincere employee needs to pay at least double the consideration it pays us. It is the level of consideration that matters. The simple term **consideration** is a complex and sensitive term, which we will discuss in a different section of this book. **This term is applicable in all types of relationships**.

Belief in God / Religion

Belief in god is the same as the belief in ourselves and others. As the saying "God is love", to believe in god is as simple as to believe in love. You pour out pure love within you to others so that it will come back to you with double impact.

Whatever be your religion, caste or creed, you need to be a lovable person so that people will recognize you, love you and moreover respect you. You need to believe strongly in your religion as well as in your god. As quoted in the holy Bible, "Let your belief protect and save you"; we all should have faith in our beliefs strongly. Then only can we achieve the result that we expect.

There are many instances where we encounter the presence of god. We may face many adverse conditions or situations resolved by others or our environment. There was a situation in my own life where I felt the presence of God. While I was working with a software company at Palakkad, a city in Kerala, our company had an assignment regarding web based projects. Some foreign books were urgently required and were inevitable for the same, and I had to take care of the matter. The books were related to engineering subjects, and the content writers to whom we outsourced the assignment were putting enough pressure to get the books.

The company from where we got the project was also putting enough and more pressure upon me to get the work done at the earliest. What I did first was to browse the net for books, the purchase of which, I found, required credit card number. In those days the use of credit cards was quite uncommon in our place. The rare holders of the same were reluctant to give their card numbers too. I was wandering like anything for the books. At last we decided to get them from abroad, for which there were a lot of formalities like getting import license and these turned out to be very troublesome. I was fed up. Lots of pressures from all the lines were flowing towards me. I was left totally helpless and hopeless.

The conditions became so worsened that without the books, lots of money would be wasted by way of expenses made so far. Also the stage had come where all the content writers simultaneously were exhausted with the stuff they had. To move their pen further, they needed to be supplied with the required raw materials. In those days technology had not been developed as it is today. The impact of globalization had just started showing up.

Feeling really helpless, I planned to quit the job. There were no further options. One night, while traveling back home from office, my counterpart and I, both working in the administration wing, stopped at a temple nearby. It was the temple of great "Parthasarathy" (Lord Vishnu) at my place. I prayed before Lord Vishnu, I cried before the Lord, I begged before the Lord. I got a slight peace of mind at that point of time.

The very next morning, when I reached office, my colleague showed me a visiting card of a person whom he met the previous night at his village. He was a person who sold books at Coimbatore in Tamilnadu. He also hinted that the said person was involved in importing books and might possess the books which we were in urgent need.

At the very instance I started to Coimbatore and met the person. By the grace of God, he was engaged in import business too and he offered to help me out. I really found the almighty before me in his form. I was really surprised and delighted to see how things went smooth by the help of God. The books were ordered, dispatched, delivered and used effectively and desired results gained and rewarded.

If you believe in God or religion strongly, it will lead to good thoughts automatically, provided you need to stick on to the principles of the same so strongly and substantially. If it is practiced genuinely you will be able to build good thoughts.

Let me state a small story to highlight the same thought. There was one who had been taken to heaven after his life. He had a chance to converse with God by revealing his life before God. God was showing him his life's path. He saw foot prints of two persons in his youth, middle age as well as old age. He asked God what it meant. God explained that in those times God was walking along with him, and the foot prints were that of him and of God. But when the journey came towards his later life, he was able to find the foot print of only one person. He came to understand that during his later years when he was sick, God left him alone and went away. He questioned God about the cruel behaviour from the side of God to leave him alone when he was to have strong support. Then God explained him that it was the foot print of God alone, and not of that person. It so happened, when he was disabled due to old age, God was carrying him on his shoulders and walking forward till his life ended. See how God's hands worked for him. We always mistake God's behaviour of such sorts. He is always there with us, offering a supporting hand. Many times we fail to recognize the same. We will get such help from God only when we do well. Only good deeds would get appreciated. So, cultivate good thoughts in your minds and live the way life comes.

Hell and heaven

Once a boy asked what the major attributes which differentiated heaven and hell were. God asked him to wait. When he was taken towards him, God first took him to hell to show him what happened there. There were many there, who were served porridge, and their hands were tied with long spoons. They were finding it difficult to have food with such long spoons. Then God took him to heaven. To his surprise, the boy could find the same situation there. Everyone had long spoons tied to their hands for having food. But, he noticed that each one was serving food to each other, and not to themselves. That made the difference between heaven and hell. What we come to understand is, we are the ones who determine our destinies. We have to choose whether we should live in heaven or hell. The decision starts right from the earth. It need not wait till we go away from earth. The cultivation of **fraternal** feeling will do that for us. The same feeling will make us think and act differently. **We fight rather than wait**. Try it otherwise and put it this way, **wait rather than fight**. Help people to lead their life. Then only will you too receive help from others. Giving only opens the way of getting.

Can we blindly believe everything?

Never ever believe everything blindly. Let me state a small story of migratory birds. There is a common habit with them to travel towards less colder areas when climate changes. On such a time, one bird lost its way and fell down somewhere. At that time, a cow unknowingly dropped some dung over its head. The bird screamed thinking that somebody was trying to kill it. But, to its surprise, the ice which disturbed it melted due to the mild heat of the dung. Now the bird felt relaxed. But, it was disturbed by the dung over its head, and was unable to get up. It so happened that after hearing the sound of the bird, one of the tigers from a nearby forest came towards it. The bird thought that it was coming to rescue it from its hardship. But it happened otherwise. The tiger ate it. On many occasions such incidents happen to us as well. Those we consider our enemies, never harm us, and those we take as our friends may harm us. Thus, do not take situations for granted. Think twice before taking a decision on choosing relationships. Also never perceive things as they appear. There is something hidden behind often. Never rely upon superficial attributes only. Just think out of the box. Never be confined to only just a framework. Come out of it and perform. You will definitely feel that there is always light at the end of the tunnel. But, the main thing is that you should be determined to walk till the end of the tunnel.

Chapter 6

Attitudes

Attitude is a term with different meanings and directions with lots of deviations too. Everybody tells about attitude, but what really is it? Attitude is a measurement of objects, people, issues etc. and has a dimension ranging from positive to negative. It is a major determinant of how we perceive things, how we perceive reality, and how we perceive the environment. It is also the major determining factor of our cognitive ability. It is really a determining factor of our mindset as well. Generally those with positive attitude will have good mindset and those with negative will have their mindsets with lots of scope for improvement.

Some people will have the real competency to perform, but will not be able to do it because of attitude problem. That means, they doesn't have the real attitude or the right attitude to do so and will fail. Only those with right attitude succeed and the rest will fail. The attitude of a person is a significant determinant of one's personality. All of us have been hearing of this very term for quite a long time. But we are confused how to develop a positive attitude towards various encounters in life. But, if you are able to develop that, you will really touch heights in life. What makes one's attitudes is a significant question at this point of time. The environment (external factors) and genetic predisposition (internal factors) determine the same. Environment means the factors which influence us while we are brought up. It may be either good or bad, which is a major determinant of our attitude. Genetic predisposition is the innate affinity or our attraction towards some factors which are beyond our conscious control. It happens unconsciously or unknowingly i.e. by our built in qualities. All of our tastes, aptitudes and attitudes are dependent on it.

A simple example is being presented before you which was elicited before me in a class room session conducted by me to a group of fresh teachers. I asked them to imagine that one of their friends had met with an accident and had broken a finger, and they are about to meet the friend at her residence. After explaining the story, I asked them how they would react to the tragic incident that had happened to their friend. Many explained in this manner: "Sir, she would really be very sad and emotionally depressed after breaking one finger. She would require strong emotional support of course. I would really cry on seeing her, sharing her pain, as a true friend".

But, I asked them what the consequence of that act would be? Would it add to her consolation, or would she feel better after meeting them. But here, I expressed them that, their approach would add lack of confidence and optimism to her instead, and it would definitely contribute to her further collapse. They agreed to my words and asked me how they should react in such a situation. I replied that they should speak to her in a manner that would bring her mental peace, and add to her confidence and optimism, and the dialogue shall be "The very sight of the accident at first gives the impression that, the rider would have been dead. The condition of the vehicle and its position after the accident really creates such an impression in our minds. But, due to God's grace, you have been saved and only so much happened to you. You have got your life back, but with a negligible negative effect on you. You have got, instead of a "miss" a real "hit" in your life". Such dialogues in such situations make huge differences. Try out and see the difference.

This "measurement" has two components:
1. **Cognitive / awareness and**
2. **Affective / emotional (values & beliefs).**

Our *beliefs* and *values* are combined with our cognitive component; thus, two components (affective/emotional and cognitive/awareness) give us our long range or persistent measurements for dealing with the world. Beliefs and values are combined to form the feelings or emotional part.

Or in other words, competencies give us the ability to perform, while attitudes give us the desire to perform. Attitudes change with various events in a person's life. These emotional changes also vary in course of time.

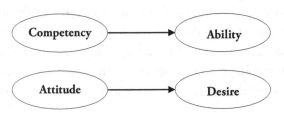

Each human emotion mobilizes the mind and body to meet one of the challenges of living and reproducing in the cognitive niche/slot.

Some challenges are posed by physical objects, and the emotions that deal with them, like disgust, fear, and appreciation of natural beauty work in straightforward ways.

Others are posed by people. The problem in dealing with people is that people can deal back.

Values

'Values' cannot be described in simple terms, because it is so complex a term that it will take time to describe it in full. But, what I would like to convey is that, all that are found good with somebody are due to his values. 'Values' differ from 'value'. But they possess some similarities too. Values mean literally value, ethics, principles, standards, morals, ideas etc.

Value could be the price, worth or importance of a thing or person. Principles could be doctrine, ideology or philosophy. All the other terms are related to the stated meanings. Thus, values of a person have got tremendous importance in building one's thoughts. They play a vital role in the building of a strong personality too. We do see many people who are being respected, and they stand out from the crowd. Why does such a thing happen? It is purely due to the values within them. Some faulty people also are getting respect and are being adored. That is a different issue. Let us not discuss it now.

People with real values are always different from others, no doubt.

Emotions

The end product of beliefs and values are called as Emotions, or in other words, they both constitute the very relevant term "Emotion". Emotions are very much necessary for our existence, via proper expression of our feelings. Our feelings are really expressed through the medium of the so called emotions. Some challenges are posed by physical objects, and the emotions that relate to them, like disgust, fear, and appreciation of natural beauty work in straightforward ways. Other challenges are posed by people. The problem in dealing with people is that people can deal back. The emotions that are evolved in response to other people's emotions, like anger, gratitude, shame, and romantic love, like a chess game obviously, and it need our intelligence and attitude to manage those.

There are a variety of emotions like resentment/ objection, strain sadness, shame, excitement, fear, sympathy, anger, disgust/ hatred, disappointment, gratitude, happiness, love, hostility etc. All of them are essential and inevitable in our day to day life.

But, emotions at times can be irritating by being problematic. This happens when someone is unable to control the extreme outburst of the same. Those who turn out as wonderful personalities have the unique quality of such emotional control. My dear readers, those who have emotional problems, please try to get control over it, otherwise it will control you, and you will be stamped by name of something related to bad personality. For such people, identify your emotional turbulence and resolve it. You can better seek the help of a Psychologist / Counsellor who is qualified and trained in helping you resolve your problems. For such disturbed people, a simple tip from my side is to become first of all aware of your disturbed status or try to simply measure the intensity of your emotions. This very awareness could help you and your therapist to resolve the issue through proper identification of your emotional disturbances. Psychotherapy can do much to resolve such problems. Thus, proper emotional control adds to one's personality in a very positive direction.

We have dissected thoughts as a product of Beliefs, Values and Attitudes. Thus, to generate good thoughts, we need to have good belief systems, values and attitudes. A healthy human being will be explained as one who is mentally, physically, socially and spiritually viable.

Habits

What is the relevance of habits in one's life? Say, one has achieved all the other three parameters of *Knowledge, Skill* and *Attitude*, but lacked required *Habits*; he will definitely end up in tremendous problems. There was a scholar, who mentored people in his society and imparted knowledge and skills to his students. But, he was not sufficiently respected by all, because, he lacked adequate habits. He was habituated with drinking alcohol, which a person like a mentor should not do. Consequently he was totally rejected by his disciples and students. Later on, he missed new students, because, their parents were hesitant to send their children to him due to his bad habits. This behaviour attracted tremendous disrespect from others.

Like wise, there are many people amongst us, who don't believe in good habit formation, and thereby lack attracting good social acceptance. There could be many factors for it, beginning from childhood habit formation from home. They might have seen their fathers coming drunk. If they turn out carbon copies of their parents, they cannot be blamed. They would misunderstand such deeds as the right habits, and later on end up in severe social problems, and at times, develop into antisocial personalities for which they cannot be blamed as well. They lack adequate habit formation from their homes. It turns to be a serious problem now a days.

Thus, good habits need to be cultured within children from their very early days from home itself. They need to be grown with good community and peers. Parents need to take extra care to resolve such issues pertaining to the habit formation of their children. Put them in such an environment where the children get adequate habit formation. As discussed somewhere in this book, negative multiples double, and positive multiples half, is applicable to habits as well. If one has particular predisposition to some bad habits, he will be doubly attracted to it, and vice versa. So we need to be extra careful while forming habits. Also, do take adequate care so that our children do not fall into traps.

Thus, habits are those which are stereotyped in us, which can be either good or bad. If we have good ones, we turn to be good and vice versa.

The KASH Model

What are ideas then?

Chapter 7

Ideas

Ideas are the emergent result of thoughts. Thoughts create ideas. Whatever we think will be converted to ideas, and dependent on the nature of thoughts. If you put good thoughts, the resultant ideas will also be good. If you put great thoughts, the resultant ideas will also be great. There are many people who rely on bad thoughts always and generate bad ideas.

That is the reason why some countries are not getting developed. The narrow mindedness of people which result in narrow actions narrows down our nation. Unless each and every one among us starts putting our thoughts in a good manner, nations will never develop. We can take another example where Germany had developed in spite of the destructions made. Like the Japanese, the Germans also worked very hard to meet success. The case of Singapore also doesn't make any difference. The thought processes of their leaders as well as citizens genuinely made them so. Singapore has been noted as a corruption free country, which we are quiet unable to even imagine. The very development of a nation thus depends upon the thoughts generated by its citizens for sure.

The spirit each and every one among them exhibited need to be appreciated. The ideas generated by them are the factors which helped them. If we discuss a very common example it will be clear. The epics, the masterpieces and the innovations we have seen so far were result of ideas. The wonders of the world and the great people are the result of great ideas. Now a days technology has developed so much that it adds to the daily needs of our lives. Years back, we were unable to think of the latest technologies like mobile phones, computers etc. which now have become inevitable things in our lives. Modern men have their mobile phones and computers just like the organs of their body. Just like our heart and liver we are inseparable from the products of technology, which are also results of best ideas.

We can say that an idea can be that valuable to change anything. Each and everything we put into practice is the result of the thoughts we have. Thus ideas are the product of thoughts. Ideas act as a buffer between thoughts and actions. The thoughts never come to immediate action without producing ideas. Thus, thoughts are being converted to actions only after they are converted to ideas.

The ideas may be **simple** as well as **complicated**. A simple idea will be like just buying provisions, going for a trip etc. A complex idea will be like creating or setting a trend, creating a nation, creating history and so on. The great thoughts of the father of our nation were converted to great ideas and when the ideas were executed properly they turned to be actions. Same is the case with epics, which we refer and depend on even now.

The thoughts of a script writer will get into ideas in the form of scripts which again will be converted to the final product in the form of a movie through his effort. Here the thoughts start from his mind, converted to ideas when it is being encrypted. It will be converted to action when it is made to a film.

Thus each and every deed or action we do, whether it is simple as moving our body parts, through a bit complicated actions like walking or running till more complex actions like trekking etc. are results of our ideas generated in the mind. These are the result of the ideas generated through the thoughts raised within our mind. Some are really confused about thoughts and ideas. They see both as same. Thoughts really start by the flow of electric signals within and from the brain.

When the signals flow in a specified manner within the brain, they form ideas, and once they start flowing outside to many organs, and the activities are done, then the action or actions are said to have taken place. Thus, the process will be Thoughts > Ideas > Actions.

Chapter 8

Actions

There comes the very important part of one's life. Just as the saying, "a good beginning is almost half done", a good thought when put into action will work wonders. This is the phase where ideas meet reality. The theory turns to be practical. Whatever we think are converted to actions appropriately. The resultant action will express one's thoughts. Thus a good action will reflect one's own mind.

"What you sow so you reap" becomes relevant here. Whatever you think is put to action with the deed you perform. Actions can take many forms like stabbing a person to construct a charity organization. The thoughts you put will make the action happen. The so called disputes, problems etc. which happen in politics and elsewhere are the results of bad thoughts.

There was a person named Viju who always worried about others' comments. He was always bothered about what others would say about him. He always perceived that others were talking about him badly and was always upset about the thought. One day he approached the king at his royal palace and presented his problem. He said that everyone was mocking at him and not giving him due respect. People were using bad words at him and showed no concern for him. He complained that some people were avoiding him while some others were asking for money.

After hearing all his complaints, the king called his commander in chief. He then asked about Viju's profession and found out that he was unemployed, and moreover didn't wish to do any work. He was found to be an idle guy who did not bother to work alone or with others. Then he ordered to place a basin full of oil on his head and make him walk through the streets. The basin was filled with oil to such a level that even a small shake would cause it to spill over. Then the king ordered that after a walk around the city, he might be presented before him if he was alive.

The order did not stop at that. If even a drop of oil was spilled over from the basin, the king ordered to take off Viju's head. When he heard the order, he was really afraid and was about to withdraw from the situation. But the king wanted his orders to be executed. Thus, Viju with a team of soldiers, with the basin full of oil on his head began to go round the city. He was so careful that the oil would not spill over and wanted to protect his life. People were really mocking at him by the sight. They were cheering up calling him bad words. Soon after an hour's walk round the city, the commander along with the soldiers ordered him to return to the palace.

He was still very careful with the basin of oil on his head till he reached the palace. After reaching the palace the king didn't ask him first whether he spilled oil or not. Rather he asked Viju whether he heard what the people were telling about him while he was on the move. He replied that he did not hear anything and told that in keeping due concentration on the basin so as not to spill the oil, he couldn't pay attention to what was happening outside lest his head would be cut.

The king then very keenly asked him whether he was sure that no oil was spilled. Viju was damn sure of it, because he put so much concentration on it to see that the disaster would not happen. Then the king told him that roaming around here and there just without any work and doing anything only invited bad comments from others, and nothing else. Thus the king advised him to indulge in some productive work, so that when engaged he would not hear others telling anything. That was the reason he didn't hear anything while walking through the city with the oil on his head even though the people were really mocking at him at his comic deed.

What we need to learn from this story is that once we have something productive to do, we would never hear anything of no use. We will be engaged in our work, and nothing else. It is only when keeping ourselves idle that we invite unwelcome things to happen to us. As the saying 'An idle mind is devil's work shop' conveys we will lose all our talents and skills when we sit idle and lose all our potentials

The above story throws light on the fact that you need to be engaged in your work more rather than give ears to unwanted talks. We don't have any other kings as in the story. As read earlier, you are your boss and king, and have full authority over yourself. You need to act keenly to refine yourselves, and bear in mind not to get into hassles.

The good actions we do will be returned to us in good ways. If you help others, in a very critical situation, it will be reflected upon you in many other forms, provided your actions are genuine. As told earlier, there will be an opposite or equal reaction for every action. You may be knowing about the instrument called boomerang used by tribes in the African continent. The specialty of the instrument is that it will come back to the person or position from where it was thrown. They use it as a weapon to hunt animals or birds. If thrown forcefully, it will come back with that much force, and if force is less the return will also be very slow.

Same will be the case with us too. What you give, you will get back.

The route is now modified as Thoughts > Ideas > Actions > Behaviour

Chapter 9

Behaviour

Whatever others perceive of your actions can be called behaviour. That is, the actions that you perform, which is interpreted by others, is called behaviour. If you perform good actions, then others take it as good behaviour from your side. Likewise if you do bad deeds it might be seen as bad behaviour also. There are innumerable theories explaining behaviour ranging from body language, facial expressions etc to various performances.

There are lots of cases coming to counselors mainly related to behaviour problems. Parents say their children behave badly and children say their parents have behavioural problems. Whatever be the issue, the basic problem will be loss of mental peace. Teachers often seem to complain about their students of severe bahaviour problems. What could be the reason? It could be very simple. It starts from the quality of their thoughts and moves through actions and reaches behaviour. So, where should we start the trimming process? Not from the bottom level, but from the top level of thoughts. The irrational thoughts need to be trimmed, which will change the overall personality. You can better use the help of your psychologist / counselor for the same.

Role of Learning and Experience in One's Personality

As we all know, one's personality is built to almost its final stage by one's learning and experience till one's 20th year. Those long 20 years absolutely determine a person's life. It has important and innumerable values. When I was speaking to a crowd of adults, I asked them, which is important, whether learning or experience. All of them answered that experience was important than learning. As per one of the internationally reputed motivational speakers, experience is more important than learning, because, experience is what you know, and learning is what you don't know. If you follow your faulty experiences without correcting them, you will not learn from them.

There was a clerk in a sales depot, who always made mistakes in arranging the departure of trucks. He used to get scolding from his boss always. In spite of all these, he went on repeating his mistakes. He had been "experiencing" the same for many years. But, if he had "learned" the required information to run the business smoothly, he would not have suffered this major set back. He was still reluctant to learn in such a fashion. Now it is clear how to differentiate between learning and experience. If that clerk had learned from his experiences, he could have performed better.

Our improvement also relies on this basic idea of learning from our mistakes. We should be open to that. Our lives should be like open books. We need to keep our senses quite open to the environment, so that, new information comes to us as and when required, even without our knowledge. To make it possible, I request my readers to acquire as much knowledge and learning as possible, from as many avenues as possible. Make reading a habit. Watch informative TV channels rather than wasting time by watching unwanted things. If you watch unwanted programmes, your brain also turns in to a dustbin, full of waste. There was a survey which brought in to light a naked truth that, by the time someone reaches adolescence, he would have acquired within him 15,000 hours of violence and the like, through TV. Hence my request to you is to avoid such habits, and accept only what is needed and useful.

As discussed, a person's personality is determined by his experience and learning till his late adolescence. Thus, if you indulge in bad company and bad information at this particular period, your personality also will be made bad, which everyone knows, will affect your entire life badly. What we see, hear and feel on a regular basis will have a hypnotic effect on our brain, whether good or bad, and will be carried over along with our personality. Our brain is like a tape-recorder. It captures things as they are. Thus, it is up to each of us to decide whether we carry good things or bad things. My sincere request to my parent readers, please take extra care not to allow your children fall into bad company. Indulge with good people and situations, whose knowledge can make you better, which means avoid bad company and situations which destroys.

Thus, be focused on your life goals, and be prepared to achieve them by adopting all positive means strictly.

Chapter 10

Problems

People often ask me "Sir how are things going?" I would answer them "Business is going good as long as people have problems". As I am in to counseling profession, I often come across various types of problems. The major problems are people problems. If we try to explain what a problem is, the apt answer would be "**Problems are differences between expectations and reality**". Either you have to expect less or be ready to face the reality. You can practically face problems this way only. Also, let me make it very clear that life itself is a continuous resolution of problems. Without problems, there is no life. We cannot escape from the problems created by various aspects of life. Just imagine a day in our life when we do not have anything to do. That means, we are supposed to sit idle. What will we feel exactly? We feel bored and feel a total uneasiness that day. What does this show? We need problems to resolve, and we are made for that indeed. That means, we are unable to escape problems; instead, we are bound to face them with confidence. Resolution of problems is an art as well as a science, and all of us need to be masters of that. There are certain problems which need not be resolved as well; otherwise, it will be a problem. Putting some problems aside unresolved also makes some difference at times. So, beware of resolving problems also. Just for an example, one runs short of money (Problem), and it is resolved (Solution) by some means, and himself turns to be a drunkard after being rich (Huge problem).

A proper way of emotional control and anxiety resolution techniques will come to our help when used properly. Otherwise, lots of emotional turbulences happen, which affect our health very badly. It eats ones psycho (Mind) and somatic (Body), which leads to numerous psycho-somatic problems.

Important among such diseases are as listed below:

Gastrointestinal disorders like Peptic Ulcer Disease, Colitis etc., Cardiovascular Disorders like heart problems and Hypertension, Cardiac Arrhythmias and Sudden Cardiac Death, Respiratory diseases like Asthma, Hyperventilation Syndrome, Endocrine diseases like Hyperthyroidism and Hypothyroidism, Adrenal Disorders like Cushing's Syndrome, Hypercortisolism, Skin disorders like Psychogenic Excoriation, Musculoskeletal Disorders like Rheumatoid Arthritis, Low Back Pain, Fibromyalgia, and Headaches etc.

Now, all of us know the inherent capacity of brain. Everything starts from the brain. Just as our thoughts, everything starts from brain, whether it is good or bad. If we experience pleasure or happiness, it affects our body positively and otherwise as well. If we feel depressed or tensed due to any of our day to day activities, it affects our body also in various means, and expresses through different bodily symptoms like head ache and fever. There was a case at my clinic, where one parent brought his boy child,

14 years of age. He was experiencing continuous attacks of fever. They had visited various physicians over a period of time, but lacked long lasting recovery. When I studied the case, most of the fever incidents were found to have occurred just before, or around the time of academic examinations. Detailed studies have shown that this boy was experiencing severe exam anxiety disorder. At times, he experienced panic attacks which would express similar symptoms of heart attack at times. Continuous counseling and intense Psychotherapy helped to resolve the problem. But, such types of issues need continuous follow ups; otherwise they would relapse as well.

There should be problems in our lives, otherwise life cannot be called life. Our lives are continuous regiments of problem resolutions, or in other words, life is a continuous cycle of problem resolutions. There are numerous individual problems as well as family problems. Aren't these problems unsolvable? Don't such problems have any resolutions? Such questions need continuous evaluation and research. We would discuss them some other time.

Depiction of Problem – A diagrammatic representation

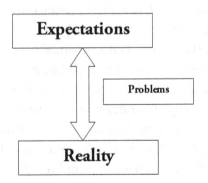

Chapter 11

Can we be positive always?

Every time we are trained to believe to think positively always. Is it possible? Let me give an example: you stand unmoving in front of a buffalo running violently to attack you. You do this because you think that if it hits you, it is for good. But this is absolutely absurd. At certain times, we need to think about the negatives first than the positives; otherwise, we will be exhausted by something called as over confidence. If you plan to start a new business, first of all you think that, the investment for the same should not be wasted, and rather, it should generate you more income. But, if you don't think like that, and invest your money in a wrong place or less potential area or in a wrong segment which you cannot manage well, would it attract profit by simply thinking positively that, whatever you do, it will succeed. It will never happen.

Similarly, when you drive your vehicle, would you simply sit, thinking that, everything will be taken control of automatically or will you control the vehicle to avoid accident? You have to control it to avoid accident, and simply thinking positively that nothing will happen, would be absurd. Here comes human capacity to discriminate between what is good and what is bad. Some people have been found to be failures, simply by thinking that whatever they do will be success, which usually never happens.

My sincere suggestion to my readers is that, think positively as much as possible

Right and Wrong

How are we able to discriminate between right and wrong, or do really "Rights" and "Wrongs" prevail? Of course it is a sensitive question to be interpreted in an unbiased way. This is so sensitive and broad an aspect, which needs to be dissected in a multidimensional way. So, at this point, I restrict the same to a limited discussion. I put before you a small incident to make the same idea simple. This incident took place in a western country, where a girl was reluctant to attend parties, and she took refuge inside her room. People perceived her as shy, and at times a mental patient. But, she was from India, where such type of behaviour was definitely treated as decent. See, something which is right for someone is being understood as wrong by others. Culture, upbringings, environment, perception levels, intellectual levels, moods etc. determine whether something is right or wrong. Something which I feel right will be perceived as wrong by others.

There is yet another story. There was a demonstration campaign regarding awareness of bad effects of alcohol in human body. The demonstrator took two glasses, in one of which he took water, and in the other, alcohol. He put a worm inside each glass. Soon the insect inside the glass of alcohol died, but the on put in the glass of water survived for more time. After this experiment, he asked the audience what they had understood from this. One of them suddenly got up and answered that, by drinking alcohol, all the worms and infectious beings inside our body would be killed by alcohol, and its consumption would genuinely enhance our health. See how positive he is towards alcoholism. This is how some people will react to some incidents. Those which are right to someone will be wrong to another. So we can conclude that there are no definite and demarcated rights and wrongs for some things, but some have it as well. There we have to use our discretionary powers to choose and follow them.

Defiant power of Human Spirit

The famous Psychotherapist and the founder of Client-Centered Therapy, Mr. Carl Rogers postulated that there is immense potential inside every human being. He is capable of resolving his problems and issues by himself. But, he has to be trained for the same. This capacity is inherent not only in human beings, but also in every living being (flora and fauna). He remarks:

> *The actualizing tendency can, of course, be thwarted or warped, but it cannot be destroyed without destroying the organism. I remember that in my boyhood, the bin in which we stored our winter's supply of potatoes was in the basement, several feet*

below a small window. The conditions were unfavorable, but the potatoes would begin to sprout pale white sprouts, so unlike the healthy green shoots they sent up when planted in the soil in the spring. But these sad, spindly sprouts would grow 2 or 3 feet in length as they reached toward the distant light of the window. The sprouts were in their bizarre, futile growth, a sort of desperate expression of the directional tendency I have been describing. They would never become plants, never mature, never fulfill their real potential. But under the most adverse circumstances, they were striving to become. Life would not give up, even if it could not flourish . . . . This potent constructive tendency is an underlying basis of the person-centered approach (Rogers, 1980, 118–119).

Thus I request my readers to spend some time for yourself alone everyday. Think about and plan for yourself. Some crazy ideas might come at times which could be utilized somewhere in your life. It might attract some values as well, and be turning points in your life.

Why envy?

In our lives we might have encountered many such instances where we feel like killing somebody. It might be to save our side, protect ourselves or to defend somebody's ideas. There can be healthy or unhealthy thoughts within us. Such killer thoughts can come to us just because of our instincts, and we don't intentionally bring them out. It can come out as actions at times, when we hear news about endless murders around us. Is it justifiable to kill somebody? Are we authorized to do it? Are we doing justice? Does it support our customs? These could be our thoughts just for rationalizations. But the fact is that, whoever is the prey, it is a great loss for his family. Their hopes are getting lost. But, does the murderer gain something? If he is a professional killer or the like, he would have made an earning out of it, but what would be his gain emotionally, socially and spiritually?

There could be many envious people around us and if we think of killing them, we need to make "killing" our profession. It is easy to kill one, but difficult not to. What I mean to say is, not to kill somebody is a difficult task, which need total emotional control as well as stability. But to kill somebody is a very easy task, which can be executed by children as well, which not at all require emotional control. Human beings, the so called intelligent ones in the world should be able to discriminate between good and bad, else we also will be like animals. Envy might be required in day to day life, but, proper control and limitation of the same needs Herculean efforts.

Chapter 12

Is there real love on earth?

Is there real love on earth? This is a genuine question I am asking you. You may be puzzled why I am asking such a question. It's really the question of the hour. Also it has to be asked to each and every one on the earth. Let me come to the point again. What is your answer? Yes or no? If it's yes, it's fine. But if it's no, you will be more right. Here it's up to you to decide the matter.

There are old age homes mushrooming now a days. If there is real love and consideration, it may not happen. Similarly pre-kindergarten institutions are also booming up. People have no time to look after their children. Neither parents nor children are getting enough love. Personal relationships are strained these days. Wherever you go or meet people, they smile at you, or rather fix a smile. The usage "fix" will be more meaningful. Everywhere artificiality is seen, and frankness is lost.

When telling about old age homes, we need to bear in mind the matter that one day we also will become old, and our children will also take us to the same old age home where we have to spend our lives leading a miserable existence, and all our beloved ones departed. What you sow is what you reap. The same situation will boomerang towards us if we especially avoid our parents. What I believe is you can get anything in this world with money, except love, trust, respect and the like.

If I ask you another question, let me see how you answer it. Whom do you love the most on earth? Again a confusing one, isn't it? You may answer it is your mother, father, sister, brother, spouse, kids etc. But is it real? Suppose it's your mother. If you are walking with your mother and find a snake just in front of you, first what will you do? Will you try to pull your mother back or will you try to safeguard yourself? This shows the selfish mentality of human beings taped inside us in the form of a response to stimulus.

No body is to be blamed. It is the prototyped or programmed feature in every human being's blood. This might also be related to the response to stimulus we discussed. Thus, each and every body will be basically selfish. What we must understand is how selfish are we? Every one needs to analyze the same thing, by asking the same question to oneself. It's the measure of our love towards our fellow beings or beloved ones.

There is a saying, living too long is as risky as dying too early. That is, if some one who is the bread winner of a family dies too early, the members of the family dependent upon him will really suffer, provided there is no alternate income for them. Same is the condition if one lives too long. He might turn a liability to the family unless there is some income to take care of the elderly. This has to be kept in mind by each and everyone of us.

How does knowledge help to generate good thoughts? To have the right belief in one's self is really a mammoth task, for which one need to have very good knowledge on one's self. He needs to be very well equipped to face the toughest things we see and feel around. He needs to possess the knowledge of relevant areas of his performance. For one to meet success it is an inevitable one. If not, it will be like a salesman selling a product without any knowledge about the product. If he doesn't know about what he sells, how can he convince a client?

To build sufficient knowledge in the concerned area would bring better belief in oneself. It will be expressed via his self confidence. Only if we make ourselves up to date in our area of concern, will we come up with flying colours. As a matter of fact, it leads to better thoughts definitely. To generate better thoughts, the knowledge base of oneself is significant to a large extent.

We see different classes of people among us who have different tastes, cultures, perception, passion, feelings and more. There are people with different styles and performances too. There are the ones who stand in high, medium and low status. Thus, all of us need to be able to build good knowledge base so that we will be able to build good belief in ourselves which leads us to build good thoughts.

Chapter 13

Needs – What are they?

As discussed earlier, we live for some "Purpose". Those who live without this blessed term will end no where. We work to achieve something, called as the goal in our life. Some work for money and luxury, some for satisfaction, and some for charity/service. But, some work exclusively for looking after their family. Needs are dependent purely on personal outlook. An important point while considering need is that, need is same for all of us, but the priority differs from person to person. If one's priority is a house, the other's may be a car. If one gives priority to satisfaction, another gives importance to children's future, and so on. If we portray our needs, we will have similar ones like those stated above, but its priority would change accordingly.

Whatever be our needs, there are three of them.

- **Basic / Emergency Needs**
- **Needs**
- **Unwanted Needs / Posh Needs &**
- **Actualization Needs**

If we are able to classify them and differentiate between them, our life will be trouble free. If we confuses between them, we would be desperate.

Basic needs are those which are inevitable for sustaining our lives, like food, water, clothes and shelter.

Needs can be something like requirement of any type of vehicle for traveling, rather than going for a posh one.

Unwanted needs will be like trying to get biryani or hamburger as food, while a simple meal would satisfy hunger. Thus, those needs are called as posh ones, which have a show off or stand a grade higher than what is required normally.

Actualization needs are those which require tremendous efforts to find self identity, or to find out what one is. It is a journey towards one's growth and development. It could be a research to discover who he is. For someone, it's a quest, but, for some, it's a thirst. It is a venue to prove what you are, to the world around you. It's a continuous struggle to meet the realities of the world in a sensible manner. This is the much demanded need, for which no body is found to be working. It is the least focused one, while most of us work for satisfying unwanted/posh needs. People drink, eat and sleep most of the time. But, how many of them work towards finding life goals or whole-heartedly help others? To resolve this question, we might require at least a tendency towards actualization, or a simple readiness for that at least.

We see saints in serene and peaceful mood, with regulated emotions, and at the blissful state of self-actualization. They have come to know the depreciation of our material lives, and meaninglessness of the mechanical world, which only pressurizes man to achieve targets. Thus we are always made to keep performing. Unless we are able to perform, we are out from the show. But, ultimately, after earning much money, if we sit and evaluate what we have done for the society, for the goodness of manhood, many of us would be in a big zero score. There lies the difference between a common man and a real saint. There is not much difference between saints and well known personalities like Mahatma Gandhi, Dalai Lama, Aung San Su Chi, Mr. Nelson Mandela. They have sacrificed their lives for the goodness of humanity.

I don't mean to say everyone should be saints, but, we have to live our lives beautifully, without being selfish. Of course, at times we may have to be selfish as well, but it shouldn't be so always. We have to live a life of service, that is, a life with a strong capacity to help and serve others. Many a time I have noticed people leading luxurious lives, hesitate to spend a penny for the sake of helping a beggar or a needy. They would always travel, drink, eat like a king, but overtly they are like filthy creatures. As discussed somewhere in this book, I reinforce the same quotation "Giving only gives way towards getting".

As a counsellor, I have earned the serene feeling of satisfaction. If someone leaves me smiling, that is the most important earning I have. My savings account will be filled with joy, happiness and satisfaction, which money cannot do for me. If each of us is ready to help someone, we could earn the same serene feeling.

Satisfaction – What is it?

We need to relatesatisfaction with problems and needs. It is nothing but, a stage of getting the same that we expected. Thus, as we discussed earlier, the level of satisfaction overcomes the level of problems, i.e., if you are fully satisfied with your environment, there will be no problem accompanying you. To put it in another words, you will be satisfied, when all your needs are met, thereby you end up with no problem at all. Here the difference between your expectations and reality are diffused, and you end up happy, with zero problems. Different people have different modes of satisfaction means. Some will be satisfied by mere earning of money, some by respect, some by love, some by valuables / food, some by trust, some by education, some by culture, and so on. Whatever it is, it is one's state of mind, and can take various forms depending upon the personalities of people. If one's needs are satisfied, it is simply his satisfaction. Thus the mandate of satisfaction depends upon what need one had chosen.

This choice creates problems as well, which acts the way opposite to what we discussed. If one has unending needs of infinite means, he will never be satisfied. Here, his expectations meet infinity, whereby he ends up in less satisfaction means (reality); his expectation – reality difference will be huge, and thereby his problems also will be huge. Thus, the choices in our lives have to be careful. The choices have to be met, otherwise, we will end up in severe problems, and their resolution could be pathetic as well.

For a dog, it runs for filling its stomach, i.e. its satisfaction. For a bird, it searches for food and grains, i.e.

its satisfaction and it goes on like that. But, if you take the case of a human being, he has now a days unlimited needs. He earns money to satisfy his needs and many times fail to enjoy with whatever he has materially earned. He works and works days and nights restlessly, sacrificing his family life and all those finer parts of his personal life, and ultimately ends up in severe conclusions in life with a huge loss of something in the form of familial love, affection etc. So, satisfaction is, as discussed, a fully choice dependent factor, which has to be done judiciously, lest you will feel it is lost, while you have almost passed your good portion of life

Some needs will be satisfied unknowingly (unconsciously), and some, knowingly (consciously), like need for food when compared to need for oxygen. The impulses whether they are controlled my Autonomous Nervous System (ANS) or Central Nervous System (CNS) make the difference.

Conclusion

Always we will be in search for someone or something to comment, or criticize upon. But, rather, if we try to comment or criticize ourselves, we make a huge difference. Some values, beliefs and attitudes really will make a huge difference in our lives as well. We are to refer the Kaizen applied by Japanese, for our daily activities. It is important in our lives, to build of a self identity or brand, so that we will outstand others. The change should happen from our thoughts, so that the resultant actions as well as subsequent behaviour could be modified. Also, knowledge, attitudes, skills and habits have got their own weightage. How we choose to believe ourselves, our friends, our organization, colleagues, relatives, God, religion etc. also make turning points in our lives. Problems are inevitable aspects of each one of our lives. We cannot always avoid them, but we can efficiently manage them by proper planning and execution. Always try to find positives in people and things, to attract peace of mind. The proper balance between expectations and reality would help in managing problems.

Use and identification of human spirit than envy really matters. Satisfaction of needs makes all of us happy. If needs are not satisfied, emotional as well as physical turmoil is the consequence. So, try to make a balance between your capacity to excel in your field and the actual practical scenario, so that, no complications come to your life. Rather than creating problems, always work for resolving them. Create love than envy in your surroundings. Proper evaluation results in exact measurement of what there is in the system. If you evaluate yourselves, you tend to find the areas where you need attunement. Thus, each and everyone among us try to change our perspectives and look forward to bring changes in ourselves; the entire society as a whole tend to change in a positive direction. There will be the end of all social evils and negativity in our society. A new rising sun would emerge in the form of reforms and substitutions. Things will change as we desire, in a positive direction, eradicating poverty, illiteracy and all kinds of social evils and helplessness. Those who need help and support would get it through the right channel, national money will not be wasted, or misused as well. The overall reform of the nation would take place if each and every one of us works towards the huge objective. For this, everyone should participate irrespective of caste or creed, gender, social or economic status etc. Humans have infinite needs, and the satisfaction of these needs demands unending efforts. There has to be a healthy balance between our actual capacity and environmental demands. If the environmental demands exceed our capacity, definitely we experience stress or tension. So, what I want to convey to my readers is that, live your life for yourself, enjoy with what you have or what you earn. If you earn much and fail or forget to enjoy with it, what is the point of earning money. Also, keep your life as simple as possible to enjoy its fruit. Along with that help somebody with what you have.